FOOD & SOUL

FOOD&SOUL

EASY & TASTY VEGETARIAN COOKERY

Food & Soul

Easy & Tasty Vegetarian Cookery

Cookbook compiled by The Brahma Kumaris, London

Second Edition 2011

ISBN 978-1-886872-16-5

Category: Vegetarian Cookery

Published by Brahma Kumaris Information Services Ltd., in association with Brahma Kumaris World Spiritual University (UK)

Registered charity No. 269971

Global Co-operation House, 65 Pound Lane, London NW10 2HH, UK

www.bkpublications.com

email: enquiries@bkpublications.com

www.bkwsu.org

Contents

Introduction

We have corn,

we have apples bending down the branches with their weight,

and grapes swelling on the vines.

There are sweet-flavoured herbs,

and vegetables which can be cooked and softened over the fire,

nor are you denied milk or thyme-scented honey.

The earth affords a lavish supply of riches.

Pythagoras

A diet for the 21st Century

As we head into the 21st century, vegetarianism is becoming an increasingly familiar part of daily life around the world. Most restaurants now have vegetarian items on the menu and a passenger can request an airline to provide a vegetarian meal. Supermarkets and other businesses are responding to consumers' demands and bringing out new ranges of tasty vegetarian foodstuffs. More and more people are choosing to become vegetarians, not just on the basis of traditional religious dictates, but out of ethical, ecological and health concerns.

Vegetarianism is nothing new – it's been around in various forms and for various reasons for many, many centuries, but its recent growth is one of the most significant changes in eating habits over the past two or three decades. Young people everywhere,

with a love and respect for all life forms, are switching towards a vegetarian diet every day. Their families and friends often begin to follow suit, and feel better for it too.

In fact, a vegetarian diet makes sense in a lot of ways. Moral, religious, health, ecological and economic reasons have motivated vegetarians over the years, and they are increasingly relevant, looking at the strain on natural resources, a variety of meat, poultry and fish-related food scares, a general concern for healthy living and a popular conscience that rejects the unnecessary suffering of animals.

With ever-greater awareness of the need to preserve natural resources and conserve the environment, people are also realising that it makes more sense to eat low on the food chain, closer to the first level of plant protein—legumes, whole grains and nuts. With so many people in the world suffering from hunger and inadequate water, a more efficient use of food resources is to grow crops that feed people directly, rather than use vast amounts of water and agricultural land for grain to feed and raise animals, which then become a small amount of animal protein on a minority of people's plates.

And if you are looking to be healthy and live longer, a vegetarian diet, especially one with a light dairy content, provides a lower or negligible intake of unhealthy cholesterol and saturated fat. Fresh vegetables, fruit and the consumption of whole grains and legumes ensure that there are plenty of vitamins, antioxidants and fibre in one's diet. High and unhealthy levels of salt, sugar, chemicals and hidden fats in processed foods are avoided. Food is

digested and passes through the system more easily, which helps prevent any toxic build-up and leaves the individual feeling lighter and fresher. Nutritional studies confirm that vegetarians are healthier and less prone to heart disease, high blood pressure, cancer, diet-related diabetes, obesity, arthritis, rheumatism, constipation, kidney disease and, of course, food poisoning.

Whatever the reason, a vegetarian is a person who has thought about what they are eating.

Three kinds of vegetarians

Along with the growth in vegetarianism, it's also easy to note that people eating a variety of different diets describe themselves as vegetarian. Vegans have the most restrictive diet, excluding not only meat, fish and other flesh but also eggs, milk and dairy products. The lacto-vegetarian eats all dairy products but not eggs, whilst the lacto-ovo-vegetarian supplements the vegan diet with milk, dairy products and eggs. All types of vegetarians exclude animal by-products such as gelatine and animal fat. The recipes in this cookbook are suitable for a lacto-vegetarian diet and include a variety of the nourishing and tasty vegetables, fruits, grains, pulses, nuts and seeds with which today's vegetarian pantry overflows.

Good nutrition and protein in the vegetarian diet

So if there are many very good reasons to be vegetarian, whether for the benefit of oneself, nature or other people the world over, are there any good reasons not to be vegetarian? The myth that a vegetarian diet is devoid of protein or other essential nutrients has long been exploded and the health and nutritional benefits of such a diet now widely accepted. Whilst it is easier to create nutritionally complete meals in a lacto-ovo-vegetarian diet than in the more restrictive vegan diet, judicious planning of the correct combination of vegetarian food for each meal will ensure sufficient protein, minerals and vitamins for all vegetarians. Nevertheless, a popular misconception still seems to be that a vegetarian diet will not provide sufficient protein. Protein can often be found in higher concentrations in non-animal sources. Nuts, such as walnuts and almonds, and legumes, such as peanuts, have a higher proportion of protein than beef. Over the last twenty years or so the recommended daily intake of protein has been reduced to about half and, for those of us not facing hunger, the problem is more likely to be too much protein rather than not enough. More details on protein appear in Useful Information to follow. As long as a diet includes a variety of grains, beans, pulses, nuts, seeds, vegetables, fruit and other produce, with or without milk and dairy products, it will provide all the necessary nutrients. Whilst people may cite taste as a reason for not being vegetarian, there are countless books available nowadays with delicious vegetarian recipes, including this one!

The spiritual element

"As a person eats, so he thinks.
As a person thinks, so he acts.
As a person acts, so he is."

This book of recipes has been prepared by the Brahma Kumaris World Spiritual University, which encourages individuals to take a more spiritual approach to all aspects of life. In common with our great spiritual, religious and wisdom traditions, the University places great importance on food. Whilst modern science tends to take a technician's approach and see the molecules, chemical compounds and nutrients that feed the body, a more spiritual, holistic perspective also places a sacred significance on what we eat, seeing how its energy can touch,

heal and sustain the soul as well. The body needs sustenance, but so does the soul; we must absorb, assimilate and integrate spiritual energy as well as physical. Practitioners of the Raja Yoga meditation, which the University teaches, are typically lacto-vegetarians. They believe that non-violence is an essential characteristic of the spiritually-awakened individual and that the essence of the human soul is peace, tranquillity and love. If the internal workings of the soul are disturbed, then meditative serenity eludes the individual. The meditator sees that whatever food is eaten has an effect on the mind, in a subtle form of the way in which alcohol or intoxicating drugs can dramatically alter mood and judgment.

When a person becomes more aware of the spiritual aspect of his or her identity, the relationship between body and soul takes on a new meaning and greater importance. The awakened inner eye of the soul gives birth to a higher sensitivity and greater awareness, revealing aspects that were previously unfelt or unknown. Subtle energies become very real and the individual is able to perceive very clearly whether something taken into the body is conducive to or inconsistent with the overall well-being of body and soul, intuitively preferring what is right.

With this perspective, food may then be placed in one of three categories. Pure (or 'sattwic') food constitutes the staples of a yogic diet. It includes fruit, grains, beans, seeds, sprouts, most vegetables, dairy products and a moderate amount of spices and herbs. Then there is stimulating (or 'rajsic') food, which may be consumed in moderation, and includes coffee, tea, colas, vinegar, radishes, spices and watermelon. Finally there are impure (or 'tamsic') items, such as tobacco, alcohol, nonprescription drugs, all meat, fish, fowl, eggs, stale food and also garlic, onions and chives. These should all be completely avoided. Ordinarily onions and garlic are recommended to non-vegetarians as blood purifiers and to help counteract the build-up of harmful animal fat and cholesterol. However, the healthy vegetarian is not in need of such protection and the spiritually perceptive meditator will be aware that they tend to arouse anxiety and irritation – passions which retard serenity and peace of mind. The purer one's diet, the more the emotions remain in a state of equilibrium, bringing tranquillity to the consciousness and greater clarity to the mind and intellect.

Consciousness in the kitchen — cooking with love!

In today's information age, we are continually bombarded with details about the physical aspects of what we eat and the effects that different ingredients may or may not have, and naturally this is important. But in this welter of information, we tend to overlook one crucial factor: the consciousness of the person cooking and the effect that this will have upon the food, and thus also on those who eat it. A cook prepares food in a physical place, but also in a spiritual or inner space. And just as the physical surroundings are best kept clean and in order, so should be the state of mind of those in the kitchen. A simple and familiar example of this concept at work can be seen in the way that home cooking, especially that of one's mother, holds a special place in our hearts. The love and care with which it is prepared more than makes up for the greater technical skills that may perhaps be found in a restaurant setting where stress, arrogance and greed may flavour the dish of the day.

When this subtle, spiritual aspect is taken into consideration, the role of the cook extends from

to be hardly enough time to cook, let alone do so peacefully and caringly, it is therefore definitely beneficial to develop a positive attitude towards cooking. Before undertaking any food preparation, remind yourself that the project at hand can and should be an enjoyable, creative activity, rather than an unpleasant, time-consuming chore. A good practice, then, is to meditate before cooking and then to let preparing the meal itself be a creative, meditative experience which yields a balanced, health-promoting diet for the body as a temple for the soul. Food always tastes better when it has been flavoured with love and happiness.

Having prepared food with this attention, Brahma Kumaris' practice is then to offer the freshly-prepared meal to the Supreme. Expressing gratitude in this way serves to enhance the spiritual quality of the food and deepen the individual's personal relationship with the Divine, while also creating a powerful, shared spiritual experience. On a very practical level, it will also help the body to prepare itself to receive and digest food. Of course, the last step is to eat, and this, too, is best done in a peaceful, unhurried and harmonious state of mind and environment; we are what we eat and also how we eat.

The information in this cookbook does not pretend to be a complete guide to nutrition or vegetarianism, which would be beyond its scope. However, whether you are a new, aspiring, partial or confirmed vegetarian, we hope that this book, with its emphasis on the soul as well as the body, will bring an added dimension to your kitchen and dining table. Cooking, and eating, should be a joyful and significant experience. So look, cook and enjoy!

simply creating tasty, nourishing meals with fresh ingredients, to including a spiritual connection with those who will be eating that food. The aim will be to touch and fill the heart as well as the palate and stomach. The love of the cook, and his or her motivation to offer sustenance, will nourish as much as the chemical components of each dish. Food cooked by a person who is angry, depressed or full of arrogance or hatred will have a different effect from food cooked with feelings of love, peace and the pure desire to serve. In other words, we are what we eat but also the thoughts and attitudes that have gone into what we are eating. Even in today's demanding society, when there sometimes seems

Useful Information

Our overall state of health, well-being and development depends, to a large extent, on maintaining a well-balanced, nutritious diet. The following contains some general guidelines for nutrition and a list of sources from which you can obtain the basic daily requirements. Once you become familiar with the basic ingredients in a vegetarian diet, it is easy to maintain good nutrition whilst also enjoying a variety of tasty meals.

The key areas are protein, B vitamins and iron, all of which will normally be present in adequate quantities in a good balanced vegetarian diet and, whilst attention should therefore be paid to them, they should not be any cause for concern.

Protein

Proteins are made up of chains of basic units called amino acids, which are used by the body as a form of structural material rather than a fuel. The body uses some twenty different amino acids to make the protein it needs. Nine of these are called essential amino acids, because they must be supplied in the food we eat, whilst the rest can be synthesised by the body. It is true that plant protein does not contain all nine essential amino acids. However it is easy to make up the complete balance of amino acids by eating appropriate combinations of food—a process known as protein complementing. This is how it works. To make a complete protein diet, combine, not necessarily in the same meal, legumes with grains or dairy products, or grains with dairy products, or nuts and seeds with green vegetables and grains or legumes. A plant protein, such as a grain combined with a pulse, will yield a high quality protein that is in some cases better than protein from an animal source. Whilst this may sound like something new, many such combinations are already within most people's diet, for example beans on toast, muesli with milk or soya milk, beans or pulses with rice or noodles with beancurd.

Legumes or pulses are dried peas, beans and lentils. This includes all soya bean products such as tempeh, tofu, soya cheese and textured vegetable protein (T.V.P.); in fact, soya by itself is a high quality protein. Grains run the gamut from barley, corn, millet, wheat, oats and rye to rice. Nuts include the familiar almonds, chestnuts, peanuts, pecans, pine nuts and walnuts while the main seeds are linseeds from the flax plant, poppy seeds, sesame seeds and sunflower seeds.

Vitamins

Whilst important nutrients such as calcium and iodine are often supplied through milk, vegetarians with little or no dairy produce in their diet should pay attention to vitamins D and B12. Vitamin D is synthesised by the skin when in sunlight and is also present in dates, green leafy vegetables grown in the sun and in small amounts in fruits. However, vitamin B12—of which only a very tiny amount is required—is believed not to be available from plant foods (apart from comfrey) and so a good vegan diet will sensibly include food products such as soya milks, dried soya mixes, yeast extract or breakfast cereals that have been fortified with it. However, both of these vitamins are supplied in milk and dairy produce and so in a balanced lacto-vegetarian diet this need not be a concern.

Dates are rich in many minerals and are also particularly valuable for their high vitamin A and D content.

Blackcurrants, citrus fruits, tomatoes and green vegetables are particularly rich in vitamin C, while vegetables in general are a very good source of a variety of minerals and vitamins.

Iron

Iron is present in dried fruits, particularly in raisins, and in certain vegetables, particularly spinach, beetroot, watercress and other green leafy vegetables. Molasses (crude sugar cane juice) and black treacle are also rich in iron. Brewer's yeast is rich in B vitamins, calcium and iron.

Grains or Cereals

Grains, also known as cereals, include rice, oats, wheat, couscous, millet and buckwheat and are the staple of practically any diet as they provide the body's basic fuel. All these cereals are a good source of complex carbohydrates and can be combined with pulses, nuts and cheese, as explained to provide a complete protein intake.

Wholegrain cereals contain all three parts of a cereal grain. The germ or inner part is the embryo from which shoots and roots emerge and contains protein, oils, thiamin and vitamin E. The endosperm, which surrounds the germ, contains carbohydrate and protein. The outer protective husk, from which bran is extracted, is abundant in B vitamins and minerals. Whole grain products are nutritionally preferable to a refined white cereal, the majority of which is derived from the endosperm alone.

1. Buckwheat - is not a grain at all, but a fruit seed of a relative of rhubarb. Unroasted buckwheat has a mild flavour. Roast buckwheat dry or sauté in a little oil for a nutty flavour. Cook 1 part of buckwheat with 3 parts of boiling water for 15-20 minutes. Buckwheat is rich in amino acids, calcium, vitamin B and vitamin E, and is gluten-free.

2. Buckwheat, roasted - is called Kasha. It has a stronger flavour and is drier than unroasted buckwheat. Cook 1 part of buckwheat with 2 parts of boiling water for 15-20 minutes.

3. Bulgur Wheat - is also known as cracked wheat. Soak in boiling water until all the water is absorbed. Cook 1 part of bulgur with 2 parts of boiling water for 15-20 minutes. It can also be cooked with rice.

4. Couscous - is the traditional basic dish of the North African countries. It is made from semolina and looks a bit similar to buckwheat. Soak 1 part of couscous with 1½ parts of boiling water. Cover and leave for 10-15 minutes. It is then ready. It can also be steamed over vegetables.

5. _Millet_ - is said to be the first grain cultivated by humanity. Before rice appeared, it was the staple food of China and it makes a very pleasant change from rice or other cereals. Cook 1 part of millet with 3 parts of cold water, bring to the boil, cover and simmer for 15 minutes. Allow to stand for 20 minutes. Millet is considered a high quality protein, alkaline, rich in lysine, high in vitamin B and gluten-free.

6. _Oats_ - are famous as a breakfast meal. Cook 1 part of oats with 3 parts of boiling water, simmer for 20-30 minutes. Oats are high in vitamin B, high quality protein and minerals, and oat bran helps to lower cholesterol.

7. _Rice, White Basmati_ - Wash and rinse the rice well. Cook 1 part rice with 2 parts of cold water, with a teaspoon of salt if desired. Bring to the boil, cover with a tight fitting lid and simmer for 15-20 minutes. There is no need to stir rice or keep removing the lid. Test with the fingertips—when it breaks, it is cooked. Drain and rinse with cold water, or the rice will continue cooking.

8. _Rice, Brown_ - Cook as above. Some brown rice may take more water and a longer time to cook. Brown rice contains important nutrients that are missing from milled, white rice.

9. _Rice, Short Grain White_ - Cook as above. This type of rice is suitable for making rice puddings.

10. _Spelt_ - has been grown and eaten around the world for thousands of years. It is an unhybridised bread wheat. It contains B vitamins, magnesium and more protein than wheat. It can be tolerated by many people who are wheat intolerant and is suitable for making bread, as it contains gluten.

11. Wheat - is in the staple diet of at least half the countries of the world. Wheat flour is used for cakes, biscuits, breads, puddings, etc. Hard wheat from the USA and Canada is usually used for breads because it is very high in gluten. Durum wheat, another hard wheat, is used for pasta. Soft wheat is used for cakes and biscuits.

12. Wheat Berries - are very tasty with a lovely nutty flavour. Rinse well, put 1 part of wheat berries with 4 parts of water, bring to the boil, cover and cook for 60 minutes until the grains burst and are soft.

Legumes or Pulses (dried Beans, Peas and Lentils)

Legumes or pulses provide high quality plant protein and fibre, have no cholesterol and are low in fat. They contain important B vitamins, many minerals such as calcium, potassium, phosphorus, iron and some also contain vitamin C. To make a complete protein, that is one providing all the essential amino acids, combine legumes with other foods, as explained earlier.

1. Adzuki Beans - are reddish brown round beans with a pleasant sweet flavour. They are rich in protein and are known as the 'king of beans' by the Japanese. Soak overnight then cook for at least an hour.

2. Black-Eyed Beans - are beige with a black spot or black eye. They cook quickly and have a pleasant taste. They do not need to be soaked overnight. They are native to Africa, but are now grown in India and China. Cook for 30 minutes.

3. Butter Beans - are large, flattish, kidney bean shaped and creamy white in colour. They make good patés and soups. They are a native of tropical America, but are now grown in many countries. Soak for 6-8 hours or overnight. Drain, rinse and cook in fresh water for approximately 45-50 minutes.

4. Cannellini Beans - are white kidney shaped beans from the red kidney bean family. They have a slightly nutty flavour and are grown in Argentina. Soak overnight and cook for at least an hour.

5. Chick Peas - (or Garbanzos) look like small hazelnuts with a light golden color. They taste delicious and can be used in salads and casseroles. They are the main ingredient in hummus. This bean is native to the Mediterranean.

6. Flageolet Beans - are an attractive pale green colour, very slim with a delicate flavour. They are lovely for salads and soups and are grown in France and Italy. Soak overnight and cook for 30-60 minutes.

7. Haricot Beans - are small, oval, white beans which belong to the kidney bean family. These are the beans used in 'Baked Beans' and also flans and salads. They have a slightly sweet flavor. Soak overnight and cook for 1-2 hours.

8. *Kidney Beans* - red or black, have a very rich flavour and kidney shape. They can be used in many salads, casseroles and chilli dishes. They are also very tasty with rice. This bean is native to the Americas.

9. *Lentils* - are available in a variety of sizes and colors, with red, green and brown most common in the West. They all cook very easily and do not need to be soaked beforehand. Some people believe that they are more easily digestible if soaked for a while. Lentils are very high in protein and have a high carbohydrate content—excellent for soups, rissoles, spreads and loaves.

10. *Mung Beans* - are small olive green beans, originating in Southeast Asia. They contain an exceptionally high proportion of vitamin A, plus vitamins B and C. This is the main bean used for bean sprouts. If cooked, they need to be soaked overnight, drained, rinsed and then cooked for 30 minutes.

11. *Peanuts* - are a legume and not a nut. They are known in their salted or roasted form, but are grown mainly as a source of vegetable oil. Peanuts contain a high proportion of fatty acids.

12. *Pinto Beans* - are speckled brown beans from Mexico, also known as refried beans. They can be used in chilli dishes instead of kidney beans.

13. *Soya Beans* - are the most nutritious of all pulses. They need a long time to cook and very careful flavouring. Tofu is made from soya beans. They contain a high quality protein and also unsaturated fats that can reduce cholesterol levels in the blood. They are the first bean of which written records are available and were recognised by the Chinese at least 2,000 years ago as being one of the main, principal and sacred crops. The others were wheat, barley, rice and millet.

14. *Split Peas* - are bright green or yellow in colour. They do not need to be soaked overnight. They make excellent soups and purée.

Preparation for cooking pulses

A. With chick peas and lentils, check for little pieces of grit or small stones before washing thoroughly.

B. Red lentils, split peas and black-eyed beans do not need to be soaked overnight.

C. All other beans and pulses need to be rinsed well and soaked overnight. Rinse again and cook 1 part of beans or lentils with 2 parts of water, according to the times mentioned.

D. Put salt with beans after they are soaked, otherwise the outsides become tough and the beans don't cook properly.

Sprouted Beans, Grains and Lentils

Sprouted beans, grains and lentils are very nutritious, rich in vitamins and minerals and contain high-quality protein. They are also very easy to grow. All you need is a wide-necked jar and a piece of cloth secured over the top with an elastic band.

Most grains, seeds and pulses are suitable, the most common being alfalfa seeds, sunflower seeds, adzuki beans, mung beans, chick peas and all kinds of lentils.

A Hotpot of Tips

Vegetables

Vegetables should be cooked either conservatively, i.e. in very little water using a tight-lidded pan (heavy-based pans are best) or as a vegetable stew or soup.

Never throw vegetable water away as it contains valuable minerals and vitamins lost from the vegetables. Vegetables should be fresh and cooked for 10-20 minutes according to variety and size. Never overcook as this destroys the vitamin C.

Cheese

Most hard cheeses are set with rennet derived from an animal source and are therefore unsuitable for vegetarians. This can also apply to soft cheeses, so always check the label. Most supermarkets and health food shops offer a good choice of vegetarian or kosher cheeses nowadays. Kosher cheeses do not contain animal rennet.

Gelling Agents

Gelatine and aspic are derived from the bones or flesh of animals or fish. Vegetable gelling agents are used instead, such as carrageen and agar, which are both from seaweed.

Spices and Seasoning

To make your own 'Garam Masala' for Indian dishes, grind together:

1 part cloves
2 parts cinnamon
1 part coriander seeds
1 part ginger
1 part nutmeg
1 part black pepper
2 parts cumin seeds

As referred to earlier, none of the recipes in this cookbook contains onion or garlic. Instead, for added flavor, a pinch of asafoetida (otherwise known as hing) may be used. As a cleansing or disinfecting agent, (e.g. to help deal with colds, catarrh, influenza and so on) use ginger, cinnamon, mustard and mustard seeds.

Thyme, marjoram and other herbs and spices also prevent and allay catarrh, chest troubles, etc.

Replacement for Eggs

The recipes in this book are lacto-vegetarian and therefore do not contain eggs. The following can be used as a replacement. For the equivalent of one egg, beat together 1 tablespoon of cornflour, 1 tablespoon of yoghurt and 1 tablespoon of milk. Alternatively, soak dried apricots overnight in water and then blend and strain them, using a spoonful or more of the resulting mixture as required. Commercially produced egg replacement products are also widely available and, as a final option, a cake may often be made by simply omitting any egg content, without substitution.

And a little history with which to end. . .

The history of vegetarianism is longer than many people might think. In fact, vegetarianism has been a part of cultures all over the world going back thousands of years. One of the early prominent vegetarians was Pythagoras, the 6th Century BC Greek philosopher and mathematician, whose community saw vegetarianism as a contribution to peace. In first century Palestine, the Essenes, a religious group of which Jesus is believed to have been a member, followed a vegetarian diet, as did many early Christians and church fathers, in a non-violent tradition later exemplified by St. Francis of Assisi. Buddhism, Zoroastrianism and Jainism, amongst other religions and beliefs, have all lent their support to vegetarianism, as well as certain groups in early Egypt. Moving to more modern times, the 18th Century Enlightenment saw a fresh appraisal of humanity's place in the order of things. Many raised moral objections to the mistreatment of animals, while the Romantic poet Shelley also pointed out that a vegetarian diet allowed for a much more efficient use of resources. A cookery book dedicated to vegetarian recipes was published in England as long ago as 1812 and a vegetarian hospital was established in 1846.

Abbreviations

Throughout this book, both metric and imperial measurements are given. The following terms are used.

C	centigrade
F	fahrenheit
tsp	teaspoon
tbs	tablespoon
g	gram
kg	kilogram
ml	milliliter
l	liter
cm	centimeter
oz	ounce
lb	pound
fl oz	fluid ounce
pint	pint
in	inch

Equivalence Table

WEIGHTS

30	g	(1 oz)
60	g	(2 oz)
90	g	(3 oz)
125	g	(4 oz)
150	g	(5 oz)
180	g	(6 oz)
210	g	(7 oz)
250	g	(8 oz)
270	g	(9 oz)
300	g	(10 oz)
330	g	(11 oz)
360	g	(12 oz)
400	g	(13 oz)
420	g	(14 oz)
450	g	(15 oz)
500	g	(1 lb)
510	g	(17 oz)
540	g	(18 oz)
570	g	(19 oz)
625	g	(1¼ lb)
750	g	(1½ lb)
875	g	(1¾ lb)
1	kg	(2 lb)
1.5	kg	(3 lb)

LIQUID MEASURES

30	ml	(1 fl oz)
60	ml	(2 fl oz)
100	ml	(3 fl oz)
125	ml	(4 fl oz)
150	ml	(¼ pint)
180	ml	(6 fl oz)
210	ml	(7 fl oz)
240	ml	(8 fl oz)
270	ml	(9 fl oz)
300	ml	(½ pint)
330	ml	(11 fl oz)
360	ml	(12 fl oz)
390	ml	(13 fl oz)
420	ml	(14 fl oz)
450	ml	(¾ pint)
500	ml	(16 fl oz)
600	ml	(1 pint)
750	ml	(1¼ pints)
900	ml	(1½ pints)
1.2	l	(2 pints)
1.8	l	(3 pints)

LENGTH

5	mm	(¼ in)
1	cm	(½ in)
2	cm	(¾ in)
2.5	cm	(1 in)
5	cm	(2 in)
8	cm	(3 in)
10	cm	(4 in)
12	cm	(5 in)
15	cm	(6 in)
18	cm	(7 in)
20	cm	(8 in)
23	cm	(9 in)
25	cm	(10 in)
28	cm	(11 in)

OVEN TEMPERATURES

120°C / 250°F / Gas Mark ½

140°C / 275°F / Gas Mark 1

150°C / 300°F / Gas Mark 2

160°C / 325°F / Gas Mark 3

180°C / 350°F / Gas Mark 4

190°C / 375°F / Gas Mark 5

200°C / 400°F / Gas Mark 6

220°C / 425°F / Gas Mark 7

Starters

Avocado and Tomato Spread (Opposite below)

Peel and roughly cut the avocado into pieces, chop the tomatoes into small pieces, mix and mash all the ingredients together, beat until smooth. Add lemon juice, salt and pepper.

Keep in an airtight container, in a cool place.

Serve with toast.

1 Avocado, peeled
1 Large tomato, peeled
A little lemon juice
Salt and pepper to taste

Cottage Cheese with Tomato Spread

Cut the tomatoes into small cubes. Put a little butter or margarine into a frying pan and add the ground cumin seeds. Allow the cumin to brown for a couple of seconds, then add tomatoes and a little salt and pepper. Cook the tomatoes for 3 to 4 minutes. Remove from the heat, add cottage cheese and mix. Return to a low flame to warm slightly.

Variation: replace tomatoes with chopped mushrooms.

Serve with rice or on toast.

220 G (7 oz) tomatoes, diced
1 tsp butter or margarine
Pinch of cumin seeds, ground
Salt and pepper, to taste
360 G (12 oz) cottage cheese (page 212)

Hummus (Opposite above)

Soak the chick peas overnight. Wash and cook in boiling water for 1 hour or until soft. Drain and reserve the water. Place all the ingredients in a blender, add the reserved chick pea water a little at a time and blend to a soft paste. Keep in an airtight container.

Note: Cook the chick peas in pressure cooker to save time.

500 G (1 lb) white chick peas
2 - 3 Tbs lemon juice
4 Tbs tahini
Pinch of asafoetida (hing)
3 Tbs olive oil
Salt and pepper, to taste

Cold Stuffed Peppers

Cut the tops off the peppers, save the tops and discard the seeds. Mix all the other ingredients together and fill the peppers. Replace the tops. Cover with cling film and leave in the refrigerator to set for 1-2 hours.

Serve with salad.

SERVES 4.

4 green peppers
440 g (14 oz) cream cheese
125 g (4 oz) cheddar cheese, grated
60 ml (2 fl oz) buttermilk
1 small potato, boiled, peeled and diced

Cheese Paste

Mix all the ingredients to form a paste. For a softer mixture, add extra milk.

Serve with toast.

230 g (8 oz) cheddar cheese, grated
60 g (2 oz) butter or margarine
½ tsp salt
¼ tsp black pepper
¼ tsp mustard
3-5 tbs milk
30 g (1 oz) olives, finely chopped (optional)

Mozzarella and Tomato Salad (Opposite)

Thinly slice the Mozzarella balls. Slice the tomatoes horizontally to make rings. Arrange Mozzarella and tomato rings alternately on a large plate. Pour oil over sparingly and garnish with chopped basil. Add salt and pepper to taste. Lemon juice can also be squeezed over.

Serve with breads such as Focaccia (page 181).

SERVES 4.

2 Mozzarella balls
4 tomatoes
2 tbs olive oil
fresh basil, whole OR chopped
salt and pepper
lemon juice (optional)

Mushroom and Walnut Paté

Fry the chopped mushrooms in olive oil, over a low heat, until tender. Blend the walnuts and mushrooms together and add soya sauce, a little at a time, until the consistency is like paté. Add black pepper to taste.

Serve with salad, toast or savoury biscuits.

125 g (4 oz) mushrooms, finely chopped
1 tbs olive oil
125 g (4 oz) walnuts, finely chopped
soya sauce, to mix
black pepper, to taste

Plain Pancakes

Combine the flour, water or milk, salt and pepper and use an electric mixer to make a smooth batter. Heat 1 tablespoon of oil in frying pan and spread the pancake batter evenly in the pan with a spoon. Fry each side until golden brown.

250 g (8 oz) self-raising flour
water OR milk, to mix
salt and pepper, to taste
oil, for frying

Various fillings can be made and rolled into the pancake:
1. **Fried mushrooms seasoned with herbs, salt and pepper**
2. **Ricotta cheese or Cottage Cheese (page 212)**
3. **Maple syrup**
4. **Lemon and sugar**
5. **Chutney or any Pickle (page 90-91)**
6. **Fruit jam (page 202-211)**

MAKES 6 PANCAKES.

Spinach and Potato Patties

Heat 1 tablespoon of oil in a pan and saute the celery gently until softened. Chop the spinach, boil it in a little water and drain it. Thoroughly mix together all the ingredients except the flour and oil.

Shape the mixture into 8 large or 16 small balls and flatten them slightly. Coat the balls with flour and fry in shallow pan in hot oil for 2 minutes on each side or until golden brown.

MAKES 8 OR 16 PATTIES.

1 tbs oil
2 sticks celery, finely chopped
1 kg (2 lb) fresh spinach OR
    250 g (8 oz) frozen spinach
500 g (1 lb) potatoes, boiled and mashed
¼ tsp nutmeg
140 g (4½ oz) Cheddar cheese OR
    Cottage Cheese (page 212)
salt and pepper, to taste
flour, for coating
oil, for frying

Sweetcorn Fritters

Put the corn in a bowl. Sift the flour into the bowl and add the salt, pepper and sugar. Then stir in the cream and mix thoroughly. Place a tablespoon of oil in a griddle or large frying pan and heat for a few seconds. Drop spoonfuls of corn batter onto the griddle or pan. Flatten them with a palette knife.

Turn the fritter over with a palette knife and cook the other side for 1-2 minutes or until golden brown. Repeat with the remaining batter, keeping the fritters warm until ready to serve.

SERVES 4.

500 g (1 lb) frozen corn
4 tbs self-raising flour
½ tsp salt
½ tsp black pepper, ground
½ tsp caster sugar
150 ml (¼ pint) double cream
oil, for frying

Vegetable Pakoras (Opposite)

Place all the ingredients for the batter in a bowl, except the water and oil. Slowly add in the water until a thick smooth batter is formed. Allow it to stand for about 10 minutes. Add 1 tablespoon of hot oil and mix.

Wash and dry the vegetables. Drain them on a paper towel.

Do not mix the vegetables as the cooking times vary.

Heat the oil for frying. Dip a few vegetables at a time in the batter until fully coated. Put them gently in hot oil over a medium heat until golden brown. Drain on a paper towel.

Serve hot with Chutney for Pakoras (page 90).

MAKES 20-25.

BATTER
250 g (8 oz) gram flour
(chick pea flour)
90 g (3 oz) coarse semolina
¼ tsp cayenne pepper
salt, to taste
1 tbs fresh ginger, grated
finely
1 tsp black pepper, crushed
1 tbs lemon juice
handful of fresh coriander,
chopped
1 tbs hot oil
1 small pinch of Eno
180 ml (6 fl oz) water
oil, for deep frying

VEGETABLES
1 aubergine, cut into thin
2 mm round slices
1 potato, cut into thin
2 mm round slices
½ medium cauliflower,
broken into small florets
1 green pepper, cut round
or in thick strips
baby spinach leaves
mushrooms
bananas

Walnut Balls

Blend together the yoghurt, cornflour and milk, then mix it with the other ingredients. If the mixture is a little dry, add extra milk. Form the mixture into balls and arrange on a well-greased baking tray. Bake at 180°C/350°F/Gas Mark 4 for 25 minutes or until brown.

MAKES 8-10 BALLS.

1 tbs yoghurt
1 tbs cornflour
1 tbs milk
150 g (5 oz) walnuts, ground
60 g (2 oz) breadcrumbs
125 g (4 oz) mild Cheddar cheese,
grated
2 large sticks celery, finely chopped
salt and pepper, to taste
2 tbs parsley
1 large red pepper, finely chopped

Variety Vegetable Fritters (Opposite)

Mix the flour and water to make a smooth batter. Add the salt, pepper, and sesame seeds and mix. Dip the vegetables of your choice into the batter. Put them gently in hot oil and deep fry until golden brown and tender.

Suitable vegetables are cauliflower or broccoli broken into small florets, button mushrooms, bananas cut into rounds, potatoes cut into thin rounds, aubergines cut into 2 mm rounds, courgettes 2mm rounds or cubed, chopped spinach, chopped fenugreek, shredded cabbage or spinach, fenugreek and cabbage mixed.

SERVES 6.

125 g (4 oz) plain flour
water, to mix
salt and pepper, to taste
1 tbs seasame seeds
500 g (1 lb) vegetables
¼ tsp sodium bicarbonate
    (as raising agent)
oil, for deep frying

....

Sweet and Sour Vegetables (Opposite)

Prepare all the vegetables separately. Heat 1 tablespoon of oil in wok, add the ginger and fry for ½ minute. Continue to fry each type of vegetable separately adding oil as needed. Add one tablespoon of soya sauce whilst stir frying. Cook on high heat, tossing and turning until crisp. Deep fry the tofu. Place the stir fried vegetables, tofu and pineapples or lychees into a large serving bowl and toss gently.

Preparing the sauce:
Heat a little oil in a separate pan and fry the ginger until slightly brown. Add the juice from the pineapple or lychees, tomato puree, liquidised tomatos, vinegar, water and sugar. Next mix a little water and cornflour together, and when the consistency is smooth, pour it slowly into the sauce, stirring all the time. Cook until sauce thickens. Taste for sweetness and sourness. Add more sugar, vinegar or soya sauce if needed. Simmer further for 10 minutes and then pour over vegetables.

Optional: blanch walnuts in boiling water. Make a batter by using 125 g (4 oz) rice flour, 125 ml (4 fl oz) water, pinch of baking powder, salt and pepper. Dip blanched walnuts into the batter and deep fry until golden brown. Mix with vegetables.

Serve with rice or rice noodles. SERVES 6-8.

6 tbs oil
60 g (2 oz) ginger root, finely grated
2 green peppers, chopped
250 g (8 oz) mushrooms, chopped
250 g (8 oz) carrots, sliced round
4 tbs soya sauce
250 g (8 oz) hard tofu, cubed
oil, for deep frying
375 g (12 oz) canned pineapple chunks
    OR lychees
125 g (4 oz) walnuts (optional)

SAUCE
1 tbs oil
1 tsp ginger root, crushed
juice from canned pineapple OR lychees
2 tbs tomato purée
470 g (15 oz) canned tomatoes, liquidised
2 tbs vinegar, cider or balsamic
water, to mix
3 tbs granulated sugar
300 ml (½ pint) water
3 tbs cornflour

Samosas (Opposite)

Mix flour, salt, lemon juice and oil in a bowl, with enough cold water to make a soft manageable dough. Cover and leave to one side.

Heat 2-3 tablespoons of oil in a saucepan and put in the cumin seeds. When the cumin seeds become dark brown, add the vegetables. Stir, cover and allow the vegetables to cook for 10-15 minutes over a low heat, stirring occasionally to avoid sticking to the pan and making sure that vegetables are not overcooked and mushy. Add in lemon juice, garam masala, salt and pepper and cook for a further 2-3 minutes. Put the vegetable mixture in a big tray to cool quickly.

Divide the dough into small balls, the size of a walnut. Roll each ball out into rounds of 8-10 cm (3-4 in) in diameter, and cut them in half. Place the filling on one half of each semi-circle. Moisten the edge of the pastry with a little water, fold over the other side and seal by pressing and twisting over slightly.

Samosas must be well sealed so that they don't come apart whilst frying.

Heat the oil in a frying pan and deep fry the samosas until golden brown.

Serve with Chutney (page 90-91).

MAKES 10-12 SAMOSAS.

PASTRY
250 g (8 oz) plain flour
1 tsp salt
1 tbs lemon juice
1 tbs oil

FILLING
2-3 tbs oil
1 tbs cumin seeds
1-2 medium size potatoes, diced small
1 carrot, diced small
1-2 tbs lemon juice
1½ tsp garam masala
1½ tsp salt and pepper, to taste
oil, for deep frying

Banana and Avocado Nut Spread

Mash avocado and banana. Mix all the ingredients together. Keep in an airtight container.

Serve with toast.

1 avocado, peeled
½ banana, peeled
1 tbs lemon juice
2 tbs walnuts, chopped
2 tbs desiccated coconut

Soups

Aubergine Soup

Fry the cabbage in oil, with asafoetida, until soft and brown. Add tomatoes and water and bring to the boil. Add the aubergines and cook until just tender. Add the coconut cream, season to taste and heat through without boiling.

Garnish with fresh herbs.

SERVES 6-8.

250 g (8 oz) cabbage, finely shredded
4 tbs oil
pinch of asafoetida (hing)
4 large tomatoes, chopped
1.8 l (3 pints) water
4 medium aubergines (eggplant), chopped
150 ml (¼ pint) coconut cream
salt and pepper, to taste
handful of fresh herbs, finely chopped

Bean and Carrot Soup

Drain and rinse the beans, then simmer them for 45 minutes in a large saucepan of boiling water. Add celery, carrots, chopped parsley or basil, and nutmeg. Cook together for another 30 minutes until the beans are tender. Season with salt and pepper and knob of butter.

SERVES 8-10.

125 g (4 oz) haricot beans, soaked overnight
1.2 l (2 pints) boiling water
1 stick celery, sliced
2 large carrots, peeled and diced
30 g (1 oz) fresh parsley OR basil, chopped
pinch of nutmeg
knob (1 tsp) of butter
salt and pepper, to taste

Lentil and Pumpkin Soup (Opposite)

Lightly sauté the pumpkin in vegetable oil for 5 minutes. Add lentils and water and bring to the boil until lentils are cooked. Simmer for 20-30 minutes and blend using an electric hand blender. Season with salt and pepper and knob of butter.

SERVES 6-8.

250 g (8 oz) pumpkin, diced
2 tbs vegetable oil
125 g (4 oz) red lentils (soaked 1-2 hrs prior to cooking)
1.5 l (2½ pints) water
knob (1 tsp) of butter
salt and pepper, to taste

Broad Bean Soup

Sauté the cabbage in oil, with asafoetida, until brown and soft. Add the water, broad beans, lemon rind, lemon juice and half of the parsley. Bring to the boil, cover and simmer until the beans are tender. Liquidise with hand-held blender until smooth.

Reheat and serve, season to taste, and garnish with remaining parsley.

SERVES 6-8.

125 g (4 oz) cabbage, shredded
3 tbs cooking oil
pinch of asafoetida (hing)
1.2 litre (2 pints) water
500 g (1 lb) broad beans, shelled or frozen
grated rind and juice of 3 lemons
60 g (2 oz) fresh parsley, finely chopped
salt and pepper, to taste

Carrot Soup

Boil the carrots and potato in water until just tender. Allow to cool. Blend the carrots, potato and water, and return to the saucepan, add salt, pepper, ginger and butter and bring back to the boil.

SERVES 4.

500 g (1 lb) carrots, peeled and chopped
900 ml (1 ½ pints) boiling water
salt and pepper, to taste
1 tbs fresh ginger, finely grated
knob (1 tsp) of butter
1 potato, peeled and chopped

Broccoli Soup

Heat the milk and water in a big saucepan, add broccoli and potatoes and bring to boil, reduce the heat and simmer for 15-20 minutes. Place the vegetables and some of the liquid in a blender, and blend well. Return the blended mixture to the rest of the liquid. Add more water if necessary. Add the seasoning and a knob of butter and mix well.

Serve with hot buttered toast or croutons.

SERVES 8.

1 kg (2 lb) broccoli, finely chopped
3 potatoes, cubed
300 ml (½ pint) milk
600 ml (1 pint) water
salt and pepper, to taste
knob (1 tsp) of butter

Celery Soup

Boil the celery in water for 10-15 minutes. Allow to cool, then blend for a couple of minutes. Return blended celery to saucepan and bring back to the boil, adding milk, cornflour, butter, salt and pepper. Continue to stir until it thickens.

Serve hot.

SERVES 5-6.

4-6 sticks celery, quartered
600 ml (1 pint) boiling water
150 ml (¼ pint) milk
1 tbs cornflour
knob (1 tsp) of butter
salt and pepper, to taste

Vegetable Soup

Boil all the vegetables until soft and retain the water. Blend the vegetables and some liquid until puréed. Sieve into another saucepan, adding the water from the vegetables. Add more water for a thinner soup. Bring back to the boil, adding the butter. Season with salt and pepper and garnish with parsley.

SERVES 4-6.

1-2 potatoes, peeled and chopped
125 g (4 oz) cabbage, chopped
1-2 carrots, chopped
1-2 tomatoes
90 g (3 oz) peas
900 ml (1½ pints) boiling water
knob (1 tsp) of butter
handful of fresh parsley
salt and pepper to taste

Miso Soup

Bring the water to the boil, add vegetables and simmer for 15 minutes. Dilute miso in a little water and add to the soup with the grated ginger. Turn off the heat and leave for 5 minutes with the lid on.

SERVES 4-6.

900 ml (1½ pints) water
2 carrots, diced
1 small turnip, diced
2-3 cabbage leaves, thinly shredded
1 tbs of miso (made from soya beans)
1½ tbs fresh ginger, finely grated

Minestrone Soup (Opposite)

Sauté all the vegetables in oil in a fairly large pan for a few minutes. Add enough water to cover the vegetables and beans. Add mixed herbs, tomato purée and soya chunks.

Simmer until all the vegetables are cooked.

Season to taste and serve.

SERVES 6-8.

2 carrots, diced
250 g (8 oz) broccoli, broken into small florets
125 g (4 oz) cauliflower, broken into small florets
2 potatoes, diced
1 small turnip, diced
60 g (2 oz) canned red kidney beans
60 g (2 oz) French beans, cut ½ inch
3 tbs oil
1.2 litres (2 pints) boiling water
1 tbs mixed herbs
2 tbs tomato purée
125 g (4 oz) soya chunks
salt and pepper, to taste

Mushroom Soup

Put the water into a saucepan with butter or margarine and mushrooms. Cook until soft and tender. Use hand blender or food processor to blend.

Add salt, pepper, cornflour and herbs. When mixed, slowly add milk, stirring continuously until the soup is thick and creamy.

SERVES 4-6.

300 ml (½ pint) water
1 tbs butter OR margarine
500 g (1 lb) fresh mushrooms, sliced
salt and pepper, to taste
2 tbs cornflour
1 tsp herbs
300 ml (½ pint) milk

Potato and Celery Soup

Sauté celery in oil in a saucepan and season with salt and pepper. Add water and potatoes. Bring to the boil and simmer until the potatoes are soft.

Add the butter, using the hand blender; blend the soup until it is creamy. Add a little milk or single cream for richness.

SERVES 4-6.

4 sticks celery, finely chopped
2 tbs oil
salt and pepper, to taste
900 ml (1½ pints) water
5 small potatoes, peeled and cubed
knob (1 tsp) of butter
milk OR single cream (optional)

Pumpkin Soup

Put vegetables in a saucepan with cold water. Bring to the boil and simmer for 20 minutes.

Blend until smooth. Add salt, pepper and butter. Garnish with parsley.

In winter add grated ginger.

SERVES 6-8.

1 small pumpkin, peeled and cubed
1 small potato, peeled and cubed
1.2 l (2 pints) water
salt and pepper, to taste
1 tbs parsley
knob (1 tsp) of butter

Spinach and Split Pea Soup

Heat the oil in a saucepan, add the spinach and cook for 5 minutes. Wash the split peas. Add split peas and water to the spinach and simmer until the split peas are cooked. Add salt, pepper, ginger and tomato purée.

Serve with rice.

Serves 4-6.

2 tbs oil
500 g (1 lb) spinach, washed and chopped
125 g (4 oz) yellow split peas
900 ml (1½ pints) cold water
salt and pepper, to taste
1 tbs fresh ginger, finely grated
½ tbs tomato purée (optional)

Vegetable and Kidney Bean Soup

Boil kidney beans in pressure cooker until soft and tender. Top and tail the runner beans and cut into short lengths. Put the water in a large saucepan with the oil and add all the vegetables. Cover and cook over a medium heat for 30 minutes until the vegetables are tender. Add the macaroni, kidney beans, salt and pepper and cook for a further 10 minutes.

Serve the soup in individual bowls and, just before serving, garnish with parsley and sprinkle with cheese.

SERVES 8-10.

125 g (4 oz) runner beans
150 g (5 oz) kidney beans, soaked
   overnight
1.5 l (2½ pints) boiling water
3 tbs olive oil
1 large carrot, diced
½ small cauliflower, broken into small
   florets
2 stalks celery, chopped
2 medium potatoes, peeled and diced
60 g (2 oz) small whole-wheat macaroni
handful of fresh parsley, finely chopped
cheese, to garnish
salt and pepper, to taste

Tomato Soup (Opposite)

Blend the tomatoes with water. Sieve the mixture through a large strainer into a saucepan and add tomato purée, mashed potato, sugar, salt and pepper. Bring to the boil and simmer for about 20 minutes, then add the knob of butter. Remove from the heat. Add the cream just before serving and garnish with parsley.

SERVES 4-6.

500 g (1 lb) tomatoes
600 ml (1 pint) water
1 tbs tomato purée
1 large potato, boiled and mashed
1 tsp sugar
salt and pepper, to taste
knob (1 tsp) of butter
300 ml (½ pint) double cream
1 tbs fresh parsley, chopped

Sweetcorn Soup

Boil the corn in water for 5-10 minutes. Blend until it becomes creamy. Return blended corn to the saucepan and simmer gently for 10-15 minutes. Add salt, pepper and butter. Garnish with parsley.

SERVES 4.

500 g (1 lb) frozen corn
900 ml (1½ pints) boiling water
salt and pepper, to taste
knob (1 tsp) of butter
2 tbs fresh parsley, chopped

Vegetable and Barley Soup

Rinse and drain the barley. Place it in a pan, cover with water, bring to boil and simmer for 40-50 minutes until cooked.

Heat the oil in large saucepan, add the cabbage and stir over a medium heat until brown. Add carrots, potatoes, celery, tomatoes, salt, pepper and the cooked barley with its water. Bring to the boil. Reduce heat, cover and simmer for about 15 minutes until the vegetables are tender. Garnish with parsley before serving.

SERVES 4-6.

60 g (2 oz) pearl barley
900 ml (1½ pints) boiling water
1 tbs oil
90 g (3 oz) cabbage, shredded
2 carrots, chopped
1 potato, chopped
1 stick celery, chopped
400 g (13 oz) diced canned tomatoes
salt and pepper, to taste
2 tbs fresh parsley, chopped

Salads and Dressings

Avocado Salad

Peel the avocados and cut into small pieces. Place in a bowl with sliced mushrooms. Pour Herb Dressing over the salad and mix together.

Serve with wholemeal bread and butter or toast.

SERVES 4.

2 avocados
140 g (4½ oz) mushrooms, sliced
4 tbs Herb Dressing (page 40)

Baby Potato Salad

Boil the potatoes in their skins until just tender. Pour Vinaigrette Sauce on top, and sprinkle with fresh chopped mint.

SERVES 4-5.

500 g (1 lb) small new potatoes
3-4 tbs Vinaigrette Sauce (page 43)
handful of fresh mint

Couscous Salad (Opposite)

Cover the couscous with twice its volume of boiling water. Set aside for 30 minutes until all the water has been soaked up by the couscous. Combine the soaked couscous with all the salad ingredients and toss together. Pour the salad dressing over the top and toss again. Garnish with basil.

SERVES 6-8.

350 ml (12 fl oz) boiled water
185 g (6 oz) couscous
1 carrot, finely diced
1 red pepper, finely diced
1 tomato, finely diced
1 small cucumber, finely diced
3-4 lettuce leaves, finely chopped
60 ml (2 fl oz) Mustard Dressing OR
Vinaigrette Sauce (page 43)
handful of fresh basil, chopped

Bean Sprout Salad

Roast the sesame seeds in a pan for 2-3 minutes or until golden brown. Combine sesame seeds, bean sprouts and peppers in a large bowl. Pour the olive oil, lemon juice and soya sauce over and toss well. Refrigerate and leave to stand for a while. Toss again before serving.

SERVES 4-6.

60 g (2 oz) sesame seeds
500 g (1 lb) bean sprouts
1 red pepper, sliced
1 green pepper, sliced
2 tbs olive oil
2 tbs lemon juice
2 tbs light soya sauce

Beetroot and Apple Salad

Wash the lettuce leaves, dry well and place on a serving plate. Cut the beetroot into small cubes. Core the apple and cut into small cubes. Arrange beetroot, apple and walnut on top of the lettuce leaves.

Serve with Yoghurt Dressing.

SERVES 3.

4 lettuce leaves
2 small beetroots, cooked and peeled
1 large green apple, skinned
60 g (2 oz) walnuts, coarsely chopped
4 tbs Yoghurt Dressing (page 43)

Broccoli Salad

Steam the broccoli depending on how crunchy you want it. Leave to cool. Combine oil, salt and vinegar to the broccoli and toss lightly.

SERVES 2.

500 g (1 lb) broccoli, broken into florets
½ tsp salt
1 tsp vinegar
1 tbs oil

Butter Bean and Cauliflower Salad

Drain and rinse the butter beans. In a saucepan, cover the beans with cold water. Cook the beans until tender. Drain and cool. Steam the cauliflower until slightly tender and cool. Place beans, cauliflower and mushrooms in a bowl. Pour Oregano Dressing over the vegetables and toss lightly.

SERVES 3-4.

140 g (4½ oz) butter beans, soaked overnight
1 small cauliflower, broken into florets
140 g (4½ oz) mushrooms, sliced
6 tbs Oregano Dressing (page 42)

Tomato and Cucumber Salad

Cut cucumber in half lengthways and then into semi-circular slices. Cut tomatoes into segments. Place in a serving bowl. Sprinkle with salt and pepper. Slowly pour oil on top and mix. Sprinkle with basil and serve.

SERVES 4-5.

½ cucumber, peeled
2 large tomatoes
salt and pepper, to taste
1 tbs olive oil
handful of fresh basil, chopped

Cauliflower and Beetroot Salad

Mix all the ingredients together and chill before serving.

SERVES 4-5.

375 g (12 oz) cauliflower, broken into
small florets, lightly cooked
2 beetroots, cooked, peeled and diced
3 tbs Vinaigrette Sauce (page 43)

Cucumber and Grape Salad

Mix all the ingredients together and serve chilled.

SERVES 3-4.

½ cucumber, diced
140 g (4½ oz) green grapes, seedless
150 ml (¼ pint) plain yoghurt
½ tsp honey
1 tsp cumin seeds, ground

Green Salad

Wash the lettuce and dry it well. Tear or cut into bite-sized pieces. Wash cucumber and slice thinly. Mix lettuce and cucumber together in a bowl. Pour Olive Oil Dressing over.

Serve as a side dish.

SERVES 4.

lettuce
½ cucumber
1 tbs Olive Oil Dressing (page 41)

Cucumber and Walnut Salad

Mix all the ingredients together. Serve chilled.

SERVES 3-4.

½ cucumber, diced
60 g (2 oz) walnuts, chopped
1 tbs lemon juice
2 tbs olive oil
1 tsp dried oregano
salt and pepper

French Bean Salad

Cut the beans in half. Steam until tender. Place on a salad dish, sprinkle with salt, pepper, olive oil and lemon juice and toss. Sprinkle with mint.

SERVES 4-5.

500 g (1 lb) French beans
salt and pepper, to taste
1 tbs olive oil
1 tbs lemon juice
handful of fresh mint, chopped

Mixed Bean Salad

Drain and rinse the beans. Place them in a saucepan and cover with cold water. Cook over a low heat until tender. Drain and cool.

Cook the green beans in boiling water until tender and drain. Place all the beans in a bowl and add the dressing whilst still warm. Sprinkle parsley on top.

SERVES 6-8.

140 g (4½ oz) each butter beans, red kidney beans and haricot beans, soaked overnight
140 g (4½ oz) green beans
4 tbs Oregano Dressing (page 42)
2 tbs parsley, chopped

Mixed Vegetable Salad

When the potatoes are cold, peel and dice them. Add sweetcorn, cucumber and mushrooms. Dice the tomatoes. Dice the pepper after removing seeds.

Blend the oil with the seasonings and vinegar and pour over the salad before serving.

SERVES 4.

375 g (12 oz) potatoes, boiled
375 g (12 oz) sweetcorn, frozen
1 small cucumber, diced
125 g (4 oz) button mushrooms, sliced
375 g (12 oz) tomatoes OR 1 red pepper
3 tbs corn oil
pinch of salt, pepper and sugar
1 tbs cider vinegar

Potato Salad (Opposite)

Boil the potatoes until nearly tender. Leave to cool, then peel and cut into chunks. Add Mayonnaise, salt and pepper and mix gently. Wash and chop the tomatoes into small cubes, and halve the olives. Mix with the potatoes and serve.

SERVES 4.

500 g (1 lb) potatoes
Mayonnaise (page 41)
2-3 fresh tomatoes
60 g (2 oz) olives pitted, halved
Salt and pepper, to taste

Red Cabbage Salad

Mix all the ingredients together with Mayonnaise.

Serve with a salad dressing of your choice (page 40-43).

SERVES 4.

250 g (8 oz) red cabbage, finely shredded
1 green apple, cored and finely chopped
2-3 carrots, grated
1 tbs walnuts, chopped
½ quantity of Mayonnaise (page 41)

Rice and Hazelnut Salad

Wash the rice and put in a saucepan. Add salt and water. Bring to the boil, then cover, reduce the heat and simmer for 30-40 minutes until tender. Rinse in cold water and drain well. Place in a bowl with the remaining ingredients and toss thoroughly. Transfer to a shallow dish to serve.

SERVES 6-8.

210 g (7 oz) brown rice
450 ml (¾ pint) cold water
75 g (2½ oz) hazelnuts, roasted and
    chopped
1 green pepper, thinly diced
3 sticks celery, finely chopped
60 g (2 oz) mushrooms, thinly sliced
6 tbs salad dressing of your choice
    (page 40-43)
3 tbs fresh parsley, chopped
1 tsp salt

Pasta Salad (Opposite)

Cook pasta in a large pan of boiling salted water until just tender. Drain. Rinse with cold water and drain thoroughly.

Mix all the other ingredients, add them to the pasta and toss.

Serve with a salad dressing of your choice (page 40-43).

SERVES 3-4.

375 g (12 oz) pasta twists or shells
30 g (1 oz) olives, coarsely chopped
salt and pepper, to taste
1 carrot, grated
60 g (2 oz) broccoli cut in small florets
1 pepper, thin strips
2-3 fresh tomatoes, finely cubed
3 tbs lemon juice

Pasta with Artichoke Salad

Cook pasta in a large pan of boiling salted water until just tender. Drain. Rinse with cold water and drain thoroughly. Combine with all the other ingredients in a bowl. Pour the salad dressing over, toss the salad and garnish with parsley or basil.

SERVES 4-5.

500 g (1 lb) pasta
500 g (1 lb) tomatoes, chopped
125 g (4 oz) pitted black olives
345 g (11 oz) canned artichokes
60 ml (2 fl oz) Olive Oil Dressing (page 41)
handful of fresh parsley OR basil
salt and pepper, to taste

Tofu Salad

Mix together tofu, nuts, vegetables and apple, and arrange on a bed of lettuce leaves. Mix together olive oil, lemon juice, salt and pepper and sprinkle over the salad.

SERVES 6.

280 g (9 oz) tofu, cubed
1 tbs fried cashew nuts, halves
1 cucumber, cubed
1 green pepper, thinly sliced
1 carrot, thinly sliced
1 apple, thinly sliced
5-6 large lettuce leaves
3 tbs olive oil
3 tbs lemon juice
salt and pepper, to taste

Cucumber Raita

Peel and roughly cut the avocado into pieces, chop the tomatoes into small pieces, mix and mash all the ingredients together, beat until smooth. Add lemon juice, salt and pepper.

Keep in an airtight container, in a cool place.

Serve with toast.

2 cucumbers, peeled and grated

DRESSING
150 ml (¼ pint) yoghurt OR sour cream
1 tsp cumin seeds, ground and roasted
1 tbs olive oil
1 tbs lemon juice
salt and pepper, to taste

Herb Dressing

Blend all the ingredients together for 2-3 minutes. Pour over the salad just before serving.

150 ml (¼ pint) yoghurt
125 ml (4 fl oz) olive oil
1 tbs fresh parsley
2 tsp fresh mint
2 tsp fresh dill
juice of ½ lemon
salt and pepper, to taste

Lemon Tahini Dressing

Blend all the ingredients together. Pour over the salad just before serving.

4 tbs tahini
4 tbs corn oil
2 tbs water
2 tbs lemon juice
1 tsp soya sauce

Mayonnaise

Put soya milk into a blender. Pour the oil in very slowly through the lid and blend until the mixture thickens. Pour the mixture into a bowl, add lemon juice and salt and pepper, and slowly fold in. Add more lemon juice if necessary for taste. Can be kept in the refrigerator for 2-3 days.

300 ml (½ pint) soya milk
150 ml (¼ pint) olive oil
2 tsp lemon juice
Salt and pepper, to taste

Mustard Dressing

Mix the ingredients together thoroughly. Serve over salad.

2 tsp mustard paste
6 tbs olive oil
1 tbs honey
1 tbs dried basil
4 tbs lemon juice
salt and pepper, to taste

Olive Oil Dressing

Blend all the ingredients together thoroughly and serve over salad.

4 tbs olive oil
2 tbs fresh parsley, chopped
2 tbs lemon juice
¼ tsp salt

Oregano Dressing

Blend all the ingredients together. Use immediately over the salad.

1 tbs olive oil
1 tbs vinegar
1 tsp oregano
salt and pepper, to taste

Tomato Purée Dressing

Blend all the ingredients together.

Serve over a savoury pie.

150 ml (¼ pint) plain yoghurt
1 tsp tomato purée
½ tsp cumin seeds, ground
1 tsp coriander seeds, ground
1 tsp honey

Vegetable Raita

Peel and cut potatoes into small cubes and boil until tender. Chop tomatoes into cubes. Slice the celery finely.

Cut chilli in half lengthways, remove seeds and chop very finely. Cut cucumber into small cubes.

Place all the ingredients, in a bowl, add yoghurt salt and pepper and mix well. Chill for 1 hour before serving.

SERVES 4-5.

2 medium potatoes
3 tomatoes
2 sticks celery
1 green chilli
7.5 cm (3 in) piece cucumber, peeled
750 ml (1¼ pints) plain yoghurt
¼ tsp black pepper, ground
Salt to taste

Vinaigrette Sauce

Blend all the ingredients in a blender. Pour over the salad just before serving.

125 ml (4 fl oz) olive oil
¼ tsp mustard paste
60 ml (2 fl oz) cider vinegar
salt and pepper, to taste

Vinaigrette Sauce de Luxe

Blend all the ingredients thoroughly. Pour over salad a few minutes before serving.

Serve over a green salad.

125 ml (4 fl oz) olive oil
125 ml (4 fl oz) cider vinegar OR
  lemon juice
1 tbs mustard paste
1 tbs soya sauce
1 tsp dried basil

Yoghurt Dressing

Place yoghurt in a bowl. Add sugar and pepper. Coarsely crumble in the cheese. Beat well. Pour over the salad just before serving.

150 ml (¼ pint) plain yoghurt
1 tsp sugar
black pepper, to taste
60 g (2 oz) Cheddar cheese, grated OR
  Feta cheese

Main Dishes

Aubergine Casserole

Cut aubergine into 1 cm (½ in) slices. Place in a large bowl, cover with boiling water, add vinegar, stand for 15 minutes and then drain. Pat dry with absorbent paper. Dip the slices in milk, then in flour combined with sesame seeds. Heat half the oil in a large frying pan and add half the aubergine in a single layer. Cook for about 2 minutes until brown on each side. Place in a shallow ovenproof dish. Top with half the mushrooms, courgettes and tomatoes and sprinkle with basil. Combine the breadcrumbs and cheese in a bowl and sprinkle half the mixture over the tomatoes. Repeat the layers, finishing with the breadcrumbs and cheese, and dot with butter or margarine.

Bake in the oven at 190°C/375°F/Gas Mark 5 for 30-40 minutes or until the top is golden.

SERVES 6.

1 large aubergine (eggplant)
1 tbs cider vinegar
2 tbs skimmed milk
60 g (2 oz) wholemeal flour
1 tbs sesame seeds
125 ml (4 fl oz) oil
125 g (4 oz) mushrooms, sliced
2 medium courgettes (zucchini), grated
2 medium tomatoes, sliced
1 tbs basil
125 g (4 oz) breadcrumbs
150 g (5 oz) mild Cheddar cheese
30 g (1 oz) melted butter OR margarine

Broccoli and Mushroom Pie (Opposite)

Mix the flour, salt, oil and water to make a firm dough. Roll the pastry out to 5 mm (¼ in) thick. Place on a greased baking tray. Steam the broccoli for 2-3 minutes. Fry the mushrooms in oil and add to the cheese sauce. Add salt, pepper, parsley and broccoli, then pour onto the pastry.

Bake at 180°C/350°F/Gas Mark 4 for 30 minutes, or until the pastry is cooked.

SERVES 4-6.

250 g (8 oz) self-raising flour
1 tsp salt
3-4 tbs oil
cold water, to mix

500 g (1 lb) broccoli, broken into
  small florets
250 g (8 oz) mushrooms, chopped
3 tbs oil
1 quantity Cheese Sauce (page 89)
salt and pepper, to taste
handful of fresh parsley, chopped

Baked Aubergines

Slice the aubergines 1 cm (½ in) thick, place in a shallow baking dish and pour the olive oil over them. Cover with foil or a lid and bake at 180°C/350°F/Gas Mark 4 for 20 minutes.

Mix the sauce ingredients and spread evenly over the cooked aubergines. Sprinkle cheese thickly on top of the sauce. Bake for a further 15 minutes, uncovered.

Serve with rice and salad.

SERVES 4.

2 large aubergines
4 tbs olive oil
250 g (8 oz) Mozzarella cheese, grated

SAUCE
155 g (5 oz) tomato purée
salt and pepper, to taste
1 tsp oregano
2 tbs soya sauce

Bean and Potato Pie

Drain and rinse the beans. Cook them, covered with water, in a pressure cooker until soft and tender. Blend the tomatoes and purée together in a blender. Heat the oil in a saucepan, fry the celery and add the blended tomato, salt, pepper and vinegar. Add the cooked beans and simmer for 10-15 minutes.

Peel the potatoes, cut them into pieces and cover them with boiling water in a saucepan with teaspoon of salt. Boil until tender. Drain and mash, adding milk and butter or margarine until smooth and creamy. Place the bean mixture in an ovenproof dish. Spoon the mashed potatoes on top and ridge the surface with a fork. Sprinkle cheese on the top and bake in a hot oven at 200°C/400°F/Gas Mark 6 until golden brown.

SERVES 6.

470 g (15 oz) haricot beans,
*   soaked overnight*
400 g (14 oz) canned tomatoes
2-3 tbs tomato purée
2 tbs oil
4 sticks celery, finely chopped
salt and pepper, to taste
3 tbs vinegar (cider, malt or balsamic)
500 g (1 lb) potatoes
250 ml (8 fl oz) milk
4 tbs butter OR margarine
185 g (6 oz) Cheddar cheese, grated

Black-Eyed Bean Casserole

Soak the beans in hot water for at least an hour or soak them overnight in cold water. Drain and rinse, then cover with fresh water and boil until tender. Meanwhile heat the oil in a pan, add asafoetida and cabbage and fry until browned. Stir in potatoes, carrots, parsnip and celery. Cover the pan and cook over a low heat for 10 minutes, stirring occasionally to prevent the vegetables from sticking.

Stir in cooked beans with its water; add herbs, salt and pepper. Add more water if necessary so that all the vegetables are covered. Stir in the tomato purée and treacle and cook on low heat until vegetable are cooked. Sprinkle with grated cheese before serving.

SERVES 4-6.

250 g (8 oz) black-eyed beans
3 tbs oil
pinch of asafoetida (hing)
125 g (4 oz) cabbage, grated
1 large potato, peeled and diced
2 carrots, diced
1 parsnip, peeled and diced
2 sticks celery, chopped
2 tsp mixed herbs
salt and pepper, to taste
600 ml (1 pint) water
2 tbs tomato purée
2 tbs treacle
125 g (4 oz) mild Cheddar cheese, grated
   (optional)

Broad Beans with Pasta

Heat the oil in a pan and cook the broad beans for 10 minutes. Add the mushrooms and tomatoes and cook for a further 10 minutes. Add salt, pepper and parsley. Mix with the pasta, sprinkle with cheese and serve.

SERVES 3.

2 tbs oil
1 kg (2 lb) frozen broad beans
125 g (4 oz) mushrooms, chopped
440 g (14 oz) tomatoes, chopped
salt and pepper, to taste
1 tsp parsley
540 g (18 oz) pasta, cooked and drained
60 g (2 oz) Cheddar cheese, grated

Brown Rice Pie

Combine the ingredients in a bowl and mix thoroughly to make a firm consistency. Grease a baking tray and spread the mixture evenly, pressing with back of a wooden spoon.

Sprinkle extra cheese on top and bake at 200°C/400°F/Gas Mark 6 for 50 minutes or until firm.

SERVES 5-6.

375 g (12 oz) brown rice, cooked
8 tbs Cheddar cheese, grated
2 red peppers
3 carrots, grated coarsely
½ Chinese cabbage or white cabbage,
  finely chopped
250 ml (8 fl oz) plain yoghurt
2 tsp pepper
salt to taste
125 g (4 oz) mixed nuts, chopped
handful of fresh parsley, chopped
125 g (4 oz) gram flour (chick pea flour)
4 tbs of olive oil

Cannelloni (Opposite)

Cook the spinach for 5 minutes in 1 tablepoon of oil, strain and put in a bowl. Mix with Ricotta cheese. Heat 2 tablespoon of oil in a pan, add pepper and fry for 2-3 minutes or until tender. Mix with the spinach and Ricotta cheese. Add basil, salt and pepper to the mixture. Fill the cannelloni tubes with the stuffing and place on a greased baking dish.

Chop and liquidise the tomatoes. Heat the oil in a saucepan. Add the tomatoes, basil, salt and pepper and cook until thickened. Pour over the cannelloni. Sprinkle with cheese.

Bake at 200°C/400°F/Gas Mark 6 for 30-40 minutes.

SERVES 6.

STUFFING
1 kg (2 lb) spinach, washed and chopped
3 tbs oil
250 g (8 oz) Ricotta cheese
1 green pepper, chopped
1 tbs fresh basil
salt and pepper, to taste
18 cannelloni, tubes

SAUCE
4-5 large tomatoes
3 tbs oil
2 tbs fresh basil, chopped
salt and pepper, to taste
2-3 tbs mild Cheddar cheese, grated

Cauliflower Fritters

Mix flour, water, salt and pepper in a mixing bowl. Beat with an electric mixer to make a fairly thick, smooth batter. Add more water if the batter is too thick. Dip a few florets at a time into the batter and deep fry in hot oil until golden brown.

Serve with cooked rice and Sweet and Sour vegetables (page 89).

SERVES 4.

300 g (10 oz) plain flour
250 ml (8 fl oz) water
salt and pepper, to taste
1 small cauliflower, broken into florets
oil, for frying

Celery Flan

Put the flour, oatmeal and margarine in a bowl and rub them together until the mixture resembles breadcrumbs. Add water to make a firm dough. Turn onto a floured surface and knead lightly until smooth. Roll out and line a 20 cm (8 in) flan dish. Chill for 15 minutes.

Heat the oil in a pan and gently fry the celery until softened. Spread celery evenly on the flan dish. Beat together the remaining ingredients and pour onto the pastry.

Bake at 190°C/375°F/Gas Mark 5 for 35-40 minutes.

SERVES 4-5.

PASTRY
125 g (4 oz) wholemeal flour
125 g (4 oz) medium oatmeal
125 g (4 oz) margarine
2-3 tbs water

FILLING
2 tbs oil
2 sticks celery, chopped
2 tbs yoghurt
2 tbs cornflour
150 ml (5 fl oz) milk
270 g (9 oz) strong Cheddar
   cheese, grated
salt and pepper, to taste

Chick Pea and Potato Croquettes

Mix chick peas with potatoes, paprika and parsley. Season with salt and pepper. Form into croquettes. If desired, roll in breadcrumbs or wholemeal flour. Fry in hot oil until crisp and brown, then drain on absorbent paper.

Serve with Tomato Sauce (page 89) and a salad.

MAKES 20 CROQUETTES.

185 g (6 oz) chick peas, soaked, cooked, drained and mashed
500 g (1 lb) potatoes, peeled, cooked and mashed
½ tsp paprika
2 tsp fresh parsley, chopped
sea salt, to taste
freshly ground black pepper, to taste
breadcrumbs OR wholemeal flour, for coating (optional)
oil, for frying

Chick Pea Curry (Channa)

If using dry chick peas, drain and rinse them. Boil them in a pressure cooker, with enough water to cover, until soft (approximately 30 minutes). If using canned chick peas, rinse and drain.

In a large saucepan, fry the asafoetida and cumin seeds in the oil. Then add the ginger and green chilli. Finally, add the tomatoes, turmeric and garam masala. Continue to cook until the tomatoes have turned into gravy. In the meantime, mash a handful of the chick peas and add to the tomato gravy to thicken the sauce. Add the tamarind water and mix in the remaining chick peas. Simmer for 20 minutes. Add salt to taste.

Serve with Bhatura (page 176) or other bread.

SERVES 4-5.

250 g (8 oz) dry chick peas (channa), soaked overnight OR 750 g (1½ lb) canned chick peas
pinch of asafoetida (hing)
2 tsp cumin seeds
2 tbsp oil
30 g (1 oz) fresh ginger, finely grated
1 fresh green chilli (optional)
2 large tomatoes, finely chopped
½ tsp turmeric, ground
½ tsp garam masala (optional)
2 tbs tamarind water (soak a 25 mm [1 in] square of tamarind in warm water. When the tamarind has softened, squeeze out the water and throw away the pulp)
salt, to taste

Cauliflower Cheese (Opposite)

To prepare the cauliflower, remove the outside leaves, break it into large florets and wash and drain them. Cook them in boiling salted water for 5 minutes or until crunchy, then drain.

Grease a 25 x 30 cm (10 x 12 in) ovenproof dish. Fill it with the cauliflower and the Cheese Sauce. Sprinkle grated cheese on top.

Bake in the oven at 180°C/350°F/Gas Mark 4 for 20-25 minutes.

SERVES 4.

1 large cauliflower
Cheese Sauce (page 89)
30 g (1 oz) strong Cheddar cheese, grated
1 tsp salt

Chinese Noodles

Cook noodles in boiling water as per instructions on the packet. Drain and rinse with cold water. Heat oil and ginger in a wok or suitable pan. Saute the carrots, add peppers and lastly the mushrooms. Add 1-2 tablespoons soya sauce and toss.

Cook for 2-3 minutes. Add cooked noodles, mix well and add 2 more tablespoon of soya sauce if necessary

Season with salt and pepper to taste.

SERVES 4-6.

500 g (1 lb) Chinese noodles
2 tbs cooking oil
125 g (4 oz) carrots, sliced round
125 g (4 oz) green peppers, cut into long strips
125 g (4 oz) mushrooms, chopped
4 tbs soya sauce
1 tbs fresh ginger, finely grated
Salt and pepper, to taste

Enchilada

Mix together all the sauce ingredients and cook them over a low heat for about 10-15 minutes.

To make the filling, drain and rinse the beans thoroughly with water and partially mash them. Heat the oil or butter in a pan and stir fry the mushrooms. Add the carrot and green peppers. When half cooked, add the mashed beans. Add enough of the tomato sauce to form into a thick filling.

To make the tortillas, rub the butter or margarine into the flour. Add the salt and bind into a soft dough using the milk and water mixture. Cover and leave for about 10 minutes. Knead well, divide into 12 balls and roll out into slightly thick chapatis. Cook both sides in a frying pan and stack up on a slightly moist cloth.

Thoroughly oil the base of a deep baking tray. Take 1 tortilla, put about a tablespoon of filling mixture in the centre and fold both sides over the mixture. Fill up the remaining tortillas and arrange them in the tray. Spread the sauce over the filled tortillas and sprinkle with cheese.

Bake in the oven at 180°C/350°F/Gas Mark 4 until the cheese has melted. Garnish with chopped parsley.

Serve hot with a crisp salad.

MAKES 12 ENCHILADAS.

SAUCE
800 g (1½ lb) canned peeled tomatoes,
  liquidised OR creamed tomatoes
pinch of mixed herbs
lemon juice, to taste
green chillies, finely chopped
1 tsp sugar
1 level tsp of salt

FILLING
440 g (14 oz) canned red kidney beans
2 tbs oil OR ½ tbs butter OR margarine
125 g (4 oz) mushrooms, sliced
1 medium carrot, diced
2 green peppers, diced

TORTILLAS
375 g (12 oz) self-raising flour
60 g (2 oz) butter
1 tsp salt
150 ml (¼ pint) warm milk and water
  (½ of each)

TOPPING
250 g (8 oz) mild Cheddar cheese, grated
handful of parsley, chopped

Jacket Potatoes

Scrub the potatoes, prick them with a fork and bake them at 220°C/ 425°F/Gas Mark 7 until thoroughly cooked. Cut in half and scoop out the flesh. Mash the flesh with salt, pepper and butter or margarine, and double cream and put back into the jackets. Sprinkle with cheese, place on a tray and bake for 10 more minutes or grill for 2-3 minutes.

SERVES 6.

6 large potatoes
90 g (3 oz) melted butter or margarine
300 ml (½ pint) double cream
salt and pepper, to taste
90 g (3 oz) Cheddar cheese, finely grated

Lasagne

Set the oven to 190°C/375°F/Gas Mark 5. Chop and liquidise the tomatoes and pour into a bowl. Add salt, pepper, sugar and oil. Spread one large spoonful of sauce over the bottom of a 10 cm (4 in) deep ovenproof dish. Place sheets of lasagne over the sauce, until covered. Add layers of mushrooms, soya mince, parsley, cheese, and white sauce. Repeat 3-4 times, alternating layers of tomato sauce, lasagne sheets and the other ingredients. Sprinkle the remaining cheese and bake in the oven for 30 minutes.

SERVES 4.

440 g (14 oz) canned tomatoes
salt and pepper, to taste
1 tsp sugar (optional)
4 tbs oil
1 kg (2 lb) pre-cooked lasagna sheets
500 g (1 lb) mushrooms, chopped
250 g (8 oz) soya mince
1 tbs fresh parsley
250 g (8 oz) Mozzarella or Cheddar cheese, grated
600 ml (1 pint) White Sauce (page 89)

Lentil Loaf

Drain and rinse the lentils. Put them into a saucepan, cover with boiling water and simmer until tender. Drain and mash the lentils. Heat 2 tablespoon oil in another saucepan; add asafoetida and the chopped celery and sauté for 2-3 minutes. Mix lentils, celery and all other ingredients in a large bowl. Press into 3 greased loaf tins.

Bake at 180°C/350°F/Gas Mark 4 for 1 hour.

Suggestion: use pecans or walnuts. Serve with salad.

MAKES 3 LOAVES.

500 g (1 lb) lentils, soaked overnight
½ tsp asafoetida (hing)
60 ml (2 fl oz) oil
250 g (8 oz) mixed nuts, ground coarsely
60 g (2 oz) sunflower seeds
125 g (4 oz) oatmeal
60 g (2 oz) wheatgerm
2-3 sticks celery, chopped finely
½ tsp sage
4 tsp soya sauce
salt and pepper, to taste
2 tbs oil

Macaroni Cheese

Fill a large saucepan ¾ full with water, add salt and few drops of oil and bring to the boil, then add macaroni and cook until just tender. Meanwhile, prepare the Cheese Sauce. Drain the macaroni, mix with half the Cheese Sauce and place in a deep 25-30 cm (10-12 in) ovenproof dish. Spread the remaining sauce on the top. Sprinkle with parsley and cheese.

Grill until golden-brown or bake in the oven at 200°C/400°F/ Gas Mark 6 for 10 minutes.

SERVES 4-5.

500 g (1 lb) macaroni OR any small pasta
600 ml (1 pint) Cheese Sauce (page 89)
handful of fresh parsley, chopped
125 g (4 oz) strong Cheddar cheese, grated

Mushroom and Sweetcorn Curry

Heat 2 tablespoon oil in large saucepan, add cumin seeds, curry leaves, green chillies and ground cashew nuts. Fry until the ground cashew nuts change colour slightly. Add garam masala, liquidised tomato and the tomato purée. After cooking for 5 minutes, add the mushrooms, corn, salt and pepper and simmer for approximately 10-15 minutes. Take the pan off the heat and add fresh cream and coriander.

Serve with rice or Chapatis (page 179).

SERVES 4.

1 tsp cumin seeds
10 curry leaves
2-3 tbs cashew nuts, ground
2 tbs oil
1 green chilli, chopped
1 tsp garam masala
300 g (9½ oz) canned tomatoes, liquidised
1 tsp tomato purée
500 g (1 lb) small button mushrooms,
  halved
340 g (12 oz) canned corn kernels
salt and pepper, to taste
1-2 tbs fresh cream
handful of fresh coriander leaves, chopped

Mushroom and Spinach Pie

Put the flours and butter or margarine into a bowl and rub together lightly until the mixture resembles fine breadcrumbs. Add enough water to make a firm dough. Roll out two-thirds of the pastry thinly and line the bottom and sides of a 28 cm (11 in) flan dish.

Heat half the oil in a saucepan, add the cabbage and fry until softened. Add spinach, nutmeg, salt and pepper and cook gently for 5 minutes. Allow to cool. Fry the mushrooms gently in a separate pan with the rest of the oil. Spread half the spinach mixture on the pastry, place the mushrooms on top and cover with the remaining spinach mixture. Roll out the remaining pastry for a lid for the pie. Cut a slit in the centre of the lid.

Bake at 200°C/400°F/Gas Mark 6 for 30-35 minutes or until the pastry is golden brown.

SERVES 6.

PASTRY
280 g (9 oz) plain flour
140 g (4½ oz) self-raising flour
185 g (6 oz) butter OR margarine
3-4 tbs cold water

FILLING
3 tbs oil
90 g (3 oz) cabbage, finely shredded
500 g (1 lb) spinach, chopped and lightly cooked
pinch of nutmeg, ground
salt and pepper, to taste
250 g (8 oz) mushrooms, sliced
1 tbs sesame seeds

Nut Roast

Fry the cabbage, mushrooms and soya mince separately in oil. Mix all the ingredients together in a bowl to form a soft mixture. Add more yoghurt if needed. Place in 2 greased loaf tins and bake at 180°C/350°F/ Gas Mark 4 for 1 hour or until golden brown.

MAKES 2 LOAVES.

60 g (2 oz) cabbage, shredded
125 g (4 oz) mushrooms, sliced
125 g (4 oz) soya mince
4 tbs oil
125 g (4 oz) hazelnuts or walnuts, ground
125 g (4 oz) breadcrumbs
125 g (4 oz) peanuts, ground
1 tsp fresh parsley, chopped
1 tsp mixed herbs
salt and pepper, to taste
60 g (2 oz) strong Cheddar cheese, grated
125 ml (4 fl oz) yoghurt

Pasta with Aubergine Sauce (Opposite)

Fill a large saucepan ¾ full with water, add salt and few drops of oil, bring to the boil, then add pasta and cook until just tender. Drain well.

Wash and dice the aubergine. Heat 2 tablespoons of oil in a saucepan, add the aubergine and stir-fry until cooked. Add tomatoes and simmer for 5-10 minutes. Add herbs, lemon juice, salt, pepper and chilli.

Mix the pasta with the cooked aubergine and cheese.

SERVES 5-6.

500 g (1 lb) penne pasta
1 aubergine OR other vegetables
2 tbs oil
4-5 tomatoes, chopped
handful of fresh parsley OR 1 tbs dried
*   mixed herbs*
1 tbs lemon juice
salt and pepper, to taste
1 green chilli (optional)
125 g (4 oz) Cheddar cheese, grated

Pasta with Ricotta Cheese

Fill a large saucepan ¾ full with water add salt and a few drops of oil, bring to the boil, then add pasta and cook until just tender. Reserve some of the hot water and drain the pasta well.

Sauté the mushrooms in a little oil, add salt, pepper, parsley and soya mince. Cook for few minutes. In a serving bowl, mash the Ricotta cheese with a fork and add 2 tablespoons of hot pasta water. Add fried mushrooms, soya mince and cooked pasta, and mix well.

Sprinkle with cheese and serve hot.

SERVES 4-6.

500 g (1 lb) penne pasta
250 g (8 oz) mushrooms, chopped
2 tbs oil
salt and pepper, to taste
2 tbs fresh parsley, chopped
125 g (4 oz) soya mince
150 g (5 oz) Ricotta cheese
90 g (3 oz) Cheddar cheese, grated

Pasta with Tofu and Vegetables

Fill a large saucepan ¾ full with water add salt and few drops of oil, bring to the boil, then add pasta and cook until just tender. Drain well. Heat the oil in a pan. Stir-fry the corn and peas for few minutes. Add the blended tomatoes and purée. The consistency should not be runny, but if it gets too thick, add a little water and cook for 5 more minutes. Add salt and pepper. Cut the tofu into small chunks and deep fry for 2-3 minutes.

Mix the pasta with the vegetable tomato mixture and fried tofu, adding extra water if necessary. Sprinkle with parsley.

Pasta should be not overcooked.

SERVES 5-6.

500 g (1 lb) pasta
4 tbs oil
125 g (4 oz) frozen corn
125 g (4 oz) frozen peas
400 g (14 oz) canned tomatoes blended
2-3 tbs tomato purée
salt and pepper, to taste
315 g (10 oz) tofu
oil, for deep frying
handful of fresh parsley, chopped

Peas and Potato Curry (Opposite)

Put the oil into a fairly large saucepan, over a medium heat. When the oil is hot, add mustard seeds and allow them to pop. Add the cumin seeds and allow them to brown. Add the tomatoes and cook for 5 minutes stirring gently. Season with the spices. Mix until the spices have thoroughly blended. Add the vegetables and water, cover the saucepan and cook on a low heat until the potatoes are tender.

Sprinkle with fresh coriander leaves.

Serve with Cucumber Raita (page 40), Naan Bread (page 182) and Pappadams.

SERVES 4.

1 tbs oil
½ level tsp mustard seeds
1 level tsp cumin seeds
3 medium size tomatoes, diced
½ tsp salt, to taste
2 tbs coriander seeds, ground
½ tsp turmeric
1 chilli, seeded and chopped (optional)
1 tbs fresh ginger, grated finely
2-3 medium potatoes, diced
125 g (4 oz) frozen peas
300 ml (½ pint) water
fresh coriander leaves, chopped

Pasties

Mix the flour, salt and oil in a bowl. Rub with fingertips until the mixture resembles breadcrumbs. Add water to make a soft dough.

Heat the oil in a saucepan, add all the vegetables, soya chunks and seasonings and cook until tender, adding a little water if necessary.

Allow to cool. Divide the mixture into 10-12 portions and form into balls. Roll out each ball onto floured surface 5 mm (¼ in) in diameter.

Place 1 tablespoon of filling on each round and fold the pastry over into a semi-circle, first wetting the edges. Pinch together to seal. Brush the top with milk, place on a greased baking tray and bake at 180°C/350°F/Gas Mark 4 for 20-30 minutes or until golden brown.

Serve with Tomato Sauce (page 89).

MAKES 10-12 PASTIES.

PASTRY
180 g (6 oz) wholemeal flour
pinch of salt
3 tbs oil
300 ml (½ pint) cold water
milk, for glazing

FILLING
2 tbs oil
2 large potatoes, cubed small
250 g (8 oz) carrot, cubed small
125 g (4 oz) mushrooms, chopped
125 g (4 oz) soya chunks, boiled,
*   drained and chopped*
salt and pepper, to taste
1 tsp dried mixed herbs
1 tsp fennel seeds

Potato and Tomato Bake

Slice the potatoes and tomatoes thickly. Alternate the vegetables in a casserole dish, sprinkling each layer with herbs, salt, pepper and butter or margarine. Finish with a layer of tomatoes. Pour milk over the vegetables, cover the dish and bake in the oven at 180°C/350°F/Gas Mark 4 for about 30 minutes. Remove the cover for last 5 minutes of cooking time. Sprinkle with parsley.

SERVES 4-5.

500 g (1 lb) potatoes, peeled
750 g (1½ lb) tomatoes, skinned
1 tsp dried oregano
1 tsp dried thyme
salt and pepper, to taste
15 g (½ oz) butter OR margarine
250 ml (8 fl oz) milk
2 tbs fresh parsley, chopped

Potato Burgers

Boil and mash the potatoes. Fry the other vegetables in 2 tablespoons of oil until just tender. Add the seasoning and herbs, and mix the vegetables with the mashed potatoes.

Form into burger shapes, place on a greased tray. Brush oil on both sides and bake at 180°C/350°F/Gas Mark 4 until slightly brown. Top the burgers with cheese and bake for a few minutes until the cheese has melted.

Vegetables can be varied according to choice.
Serve with bread rolls and a salad.

MAKES 25 BURGERS.

500 g (1 lb) potatoes, peeled and quartered
250 g (8 oz) mixed frozen vegetables
125 g (4 oz) mushrooms, finely chopped
60 g (2 oz) cabbage, finely chopped
60 g (2 oz) spinach, finely chopped
2 tbs oil
salt and pepper, to taste
herbs, to taste (optional)
oil
220 g (7 oz) mild Cheddar cheese, grated

Potato Curry

Heat the oil in a saucepan, add cumin seeds, mustard seeds and asafoetida. When the seeds pop, add the potatoes, salt and turmeric. Toss the potatoes in the pan, cover and cook for a few minutes on a very low heat, stirring from time to time to prevent sticking and burning. When the potatoes are half cooked, add tomatoes, ground coriander, ground cumin, chilli and warm water. Cover the pan and cook until the potatoes are soft and well cooked. Add the lemon juice, simmer for 1 minute and turn off the heat. Garnish with chopped coriander leaves and serve hot with chapatis, puri, bread or rice.

The amount of water can be increased for more sauce or reduced as required. You can even mash a few pieces of potato and add them to thicken the sauce.

SERVES 4.

2½ - 3 tbs oil
½ tsp cumin seeds
½ tsp mustard seeds
pinch of asafoetida (hing) (optional)
500 g (1 lb) potatoes, peeled and diced
salt, to taste
½ tsp turmeric powder
180 g (6 oz) tomatoes, chopped
1 tbs coriander seeds, ground
1 tbs cumin seeds, ground
1 chilli, chopped (optional)
150 ml (¼ pint) warm water
1 tsp lemon juice
coriander leaves, chopped

Yeast Free Pizza

Mix the flour, salt and oil. Add enough water to make in to a soft pliable dough. Make into 6-8 balls and roll out on a floured board to about 5mm (1/4 inch) thick. Place on an oiled baking sheet. Keep aside. Mix all the sauce ingredients and cook just for a few minutes to bring out the flavours of the herbs and spices. (Note- If the sauce is very runny, add the cornflour paste, stirring continuously). Allow to cool.

Evenly spread some of the sauce (2 tablespoon or as required) on a pizza base. Put any of the topping from the list below, ending with the grated cheese topped with a few slices of tomatoes for decoration. Sprinkle with a large pinch of oregano. Prepare as many pizzas as can be baked in the oven in one go. Bake in a hot oven at 200°C/400°F/Gas Mark 6 for 20 minutes or until the cheese has melted and the base is cooked. Whilst the pizzas are cooking prepare the remaining bases.

Serve hot with a fresh green salad. MAKES 6-8 medium pizzas.

TOPPING: (choose any from the list below to create a pizza of your choice)
Sliced mushrooms, red and green peppers - either sliced to one inch strips or cut in to 1cm square piece - canned pineapple cubes, sweet corn - can use canned or frozen which has been thawed - green/black olives (stoned), mozzarella cheese, chopped or sliced, and/or vegetarian cheddar cheese, grated. Decorate with sliced tomatoes and green or red chillies if liked.

BASE
500 g (1lb) Self raising flour
1 level tsp Salt
4 tbs Oil
Cold water to make the dough

SAUCE
400g (14oz) can of chopped tomatoes
2 tbs oil
Salt and pepper to taste
2 tsp oregano
1 tsp sugar (optional)
1 tbs cornflour mixed with 1 tbs of cold water (optional)

Wholemeal Pizza Base

Mix the flour, yeast, sugar, salt and oil; add enough luke warm water to make soft pliable dough. Cover the dough with a damp tea towel and leave in a warm place until risen to double in size. Knead well. Make 6-8 balls from the dough and roll out on a floured board to about 5mm (1/4 inch) thick. Place on an oiled baking sheet. Keep on one side until the base has risen. Bake in hot oven at 200°C/400°F/Gas Mark 6.

If you prefer crispy pizzas, you can pre-cook the base a little in a hot oven for 5 minutes before spreading the sauce and topping with other ingredients.

Prepare the sauce and the final assembling & baking as for the yeast free pizzas, above. **Serve hot with a fresh green salad.**

MAKES 6-8 MEDIUM PIZZAS

BASE
500 g (1 lb) wholemeal flour
2 level teasp Salt
2 rounded tsp sugar
3 level tsp instant dried yeast
4 tbs Oil
Warm water to make the dough

Yoghurt Pizza Base

Mix the flour and oil. Stir in the yoghurt to form soft dough. Cover and leave in a warm place for 1-2 hours.

Meanwhile, make the sauce by mixing the oil, tomatoes, herbs and seasonings together.

Knead dough well, divide into 2, roll into 2 large circles, place on greased pizza trays. Spread the sauce over the dough. Garnish with olives, mushrooms and cheese.

Bake at 200°C/425°F/Gas Mark 6 for 20-25 minutes.

Serve with a salad.

SERVES 6.

BASE
360 g (12 oz) self-raising flour
100 ml (3 fl oz) oil
4 tbs yoghurt

SAUCE
4 tbs oil
400 g (13 oz) canned chopped tomatoes
2 tbs oregano
1 tbs basil
salt and pepper, to taste

TOPPING
black olives, stoned and sliced
250 g (8 oz) mushrooms, sliced
155 g (5 oz) Mozzarella cheese, grated

Potato Pie

Sift the flour, baking powder and salt together into a mixing bowl. Melt the butter or margarine, pour into the flour and mix well. Add enough water to make a firm dough. Roll out the pastry and line a flan dish.

Prick the pastry with fork before baking. Bake at 200°C/400°F/ Gas Mark 6 for approximately 10 minutes or until golden brown.

Add the cream to the potatoes. Cook the spinach in a little oil, then mix with the potatoes and add salt and pepper. Spoon the mixture onto the half-cooked pastry base. Sprinkle sesame seeds on top and bake for a further 15-20 minutes.

SERVES 6.

PASTRY
250 g (8 oz) plain flour
1 tsp baking powder
½ tsp salt
125 g (4 oz) butter OR margarine
cold water, to mix

FILLING
125 ml (4 fl oz) single cream
4 medium sized potatoes, boiled and mashed
250 g (8 oz) spinach, chopped
1 tbs of oil
salt and pepper, to taste
1 tbs sesame seeds

Pumpkin Pie

Mix the flour, salt and butter or margarine adding the lemon juice and water a little at a time to form a firm dough. Roll out to the size of a baking dish. Prick the pastry with fork. Bake at 160°C/325°F/Gas Mark 3 for 20 minutes.

Melt half the butter or margarine and fry the cashew nuts until golden and set aside. Peel the pumpkin, remove the seeds and chop into squares. Microwave or steam until tender. Purée or mash the pumpkin and add remaining butter or margarine, then add the cashew nuts, tomato purée, spices, herbs, honey, cream or milk and cornflour. Mix thoroughly. Pour mixture onto the base. Top with cheese and herbs.

Bake at 200°C/400°F/Gas Mark 6 until golden brown on top.

SERVES 4-5.

BASE
360 g (12 oz) plain flour
1 tsp salt
210 g (7 oz) butter OR margarine
water, to mix
3 tbs lemon juice

FILLING
90 g (3 oz) butter OR margarine
60 g (2 oz) cashew nuts
1 large pumpkin
2 tbs tomato purée
1 tbs black pepper, crushed
pinch of salt
½ tbs cardamom, crushed
½ tbs cumin, roasted and crushed
1 tbs oregano
1 tbs basil
1 tbs honey
300 ml (½ pint) cream OR milk
1 tbs cornflour

TOPPING
125 g (4 oz) Cheddar cheese, grated
½ tbs oregano
½ tbs mixed herbs

Rice and Vegetable Bake

Sauté vegetables in oil for 10 minutes. Combine vegetables, cooked rice, oats and soya sauce and mix thoroughly. Add a little warm water if too dry. Transfer to a greased baking tray or tin. Sprinkle sunflower seeds on top and bake at 200°C/400°F/Gas Mark 6 for 20-25 minutes.

Serve with a sauce of your choice (page 88-89).

SERVES 4-5.

2-3 medium sized carrots, diced
2 medium potatoes – diced into small cubes
½ cauliflower, diced
Handful of shredded cabbage
2 tbs oil
250 g (8 oz) brown rice, cooked
125 g (4 oz) rolled oats
2 tbs soya sauce
30 g (1 oz) sunflower seeds

Rice with French Beans

Combine beans, cooked rice, oats, oil and soya sauce and mix thoroughly. Add a little warm water if too dry. Transfer to a greased baking tray or tin. Sprinkle sunflower seeds on top and bake at 200°C/400°F/Gas Mark 6 for 30 minutes.

Serve with a sauce of your choice (page 88-89).

SERVES 4-5.

170 g (6 oz) French beans, chopped and boiled
2 tbs oil
250 g (8 oz) brown rice, cooked
125 g (4 oz) rolled oats
2 tbs soya sauce
30 g (1 oz) sunflower seeds

Savoury Pancakes

Mix all the dry ingredients together, add water or milk and beat with a fork for 5 minutes, to make into smooth batter. Heat 1 tablespoon of oil in a heavy frying pan. Pour in a large spoonful of batter, and cook each pancake on both sides for 1-2 minutes or until golden brown.

Saute all the filling ingredients in oil. Cook until all the vegetables are soft. Allow to cool slightly, then roll the filling into the pancake.

Serve hot with Tomato Sauce (page 89).

SERVES 6.

PANCAKE
250 g (8 oz) self-raising flour
1 tsp salt
water OR milk
oil, for frying

FILLING
1 carrot, grated
60 g (2 oz) mushrooms, chopped
salt and pepper, to taste
1 tbs fresh parsley, chopped
1-2 tbs oil

Spaghetti Bolognese (Opposite)

Fill a large saucepan ¾ full with water, add salt and a few drops of oil, bring to the boil, then add spaghetti and cook until just tender. Drain well. Prepare the sauce by heating the oil in a saucepan and stir-fry the mushrooms and soya mince for a few minutes. Add the liquidised tomatoes, salt, pepper and basil and simmer for 10 minutes. The sauce should be fairly thick. To serve, put spaghetti on a plate, pour some sauce over and sprinkle cheese on top.

SERVES 4.

500 g (1 lb) spaghetti
2 tbs olive oil
250 g (8 oz) mushrooms, sliced
90 g (3 oz) soya mince
400 g (13 oz) canned tomatoes, liquidised
salt and pepper, to taste
2 tbs dried basil OR handful of fresh basil
125 g (4 oz) Cheddar cheese, grated

Spaghetti Bolognese and Soya Mince Bake

Mix cooked spaghetti with Bolognese sauce. Place in an ovenproof dish and pour cheese sauce on top. Sprinkle with cheese and fresh basil, and bake in the oven at 200°C/400°F/Gas Mark 6 for 15 minutes until golden brown.

SERVES 2-4.

sauce ingredients as Spaghetti Bolognese (page 70)
½ quantity Cheese Sauce (page 89)
125 g (4 oz) Cheddar cheese, grated
2 tbs dried basil OR handful of fresh basil

Soya Burgers

Place the soya mince in a bowl and cover with boiling water. Leave to stand for 10 minutes or until all the water is absorbed. Then add the carrot, potatoes, peanut butter or tahini, peppers, cabbage, salt and pepper. Add herbs or spices of your choice. Mix to make a firm dough. If the dough is too soft, add a little flour. Take small amounts of dough and make it into burger shapes and fry in a shallow frying pan until brown on both sides, or brush with oil and bake in the oven at 190°C/375°F/Gas Mark 5 until brown.

Serve with Tomato Sauce (page 89) and a salad.

SERVES 10-12.

125 g (4 oz) soya mince
400 ml hot water
1 carrot, grated
2-3 medium sized potatoes, cooked, peeled and mashed
60 g (2 oz) peanut butter OR tahini
1-2 peppers, chopped
60 g (2 oz) cabbage, grated
salt and pepper, to taste
1-2 tsp herbs OR spices, (optional)
oil, for frying

Spicy Burgers

Rinse and drain the beans. Cover them with cold water in a pan. Bring to boil and continue boiling rapidly for 10 minutes. Cover and simmer for 1 hour or until tender. Drain well and mash. Stir-fry the green pepper, celery, walnuts and carrots in oil for 3-4 minutes. Add the soya sauce, chillies and parsley and mix all ingredients together. Shape into 8 balls. Flatten to about 1 cm (½ in) thick. Coat the burgers with breadcrumbs and fry in hot shallow oil until golden brown on both sides.

Serve with Tomato Sauce (page 89) and a salad.

MAKES 8 BURGERS.

250 g (8 oz) black eyed beans, soaked overnight
1 green pepper, finely chopped
1 stick celery, finely chopped
60 g (2 oz) walnuts, chopped
2 carrots, grated
2 tbs oil
1 tbs soya sauce
2 chillies (optional)
2 tbs parsley, chopped
60 g (2 oz) wholemeal breadcrumbs, mixed with 1 tsp dried/fresh herbs
oil, for frying

Spinach Flan

Set the oven to 180°C/350°F/Gas Mark 4.

Line a 20 cm (8 in) flan tin. Roll out the pastry on a lightly floured surface and use to line the tin. Prick the base lightly with a fork. Melt the butter or margarine in a medium sized saucepan. Add the spinach, cover and cook very gently for 7 minutes, stirring occasionally. Add salt and pepper. If using fresh spinach, cook on high heat until the water is reduced to almost nothing. Drain thoroughly only if using frozen spinach. Mix yoghurt and cheese together and season well. Stir in the spinach and mix thoroughly. Spread mixture over the base of the flan.

Bake for 25-30 minutes until set and lightly browned.

Serve with a salad.

SERVES 4-5.

250 g (8 oz) Shortcrust Pastry
flour, for rolling
30 g (1 oz) butter OR margarine
1 kg (2 lb) fresh spinach chopped or frozen
salt and pepper, to taste
150 ml (¼ pint) plain yoghurt
185 g (6 oz) Cheddar cheese, grated

Spinach Pie (Opposite)

Heat half the oil in a saucepan. Add the spinach, stir, cover and cook for 10-15 minutes stirring occasionally. Fry the mushrooms separately with the remainder of the oil. Drain the spinach (keep the water for a healthy vitamin enriched juice or stock) and mix with salt, pepper, fried mushrooms and cottage cheese.

Sift the flour and salt into a bowl. Rub in the margarine and add water to make a soft dough. Roll the dough out to 1 cm (½ in) thick on a floured board. Grease a 25 x 30 cm (10 x 12 in) ovenproof dish. Place the rolled pastry in the dish and prick with a fork, spread the spinach mixture evenly on top. Sprinkle with grated cheese and sesame seeds.

Bake on the middle shelf at 190°C/375°F/Gas Mark 5 for 20 minutes or until golden brown.

Serve with baked potatoes and a salad.

SERVES 4.

FILLING
3 tbs oil
1.5 kg (3 lb) fresh spinach, washed and chopped
250 g (8 oz) mushrooms, sliced
salt and pepper, to taste
250 g (8 oz) plain cottage cheese
fresh parsley, chopped
90 g (3 oz) Cheddar cheese, grated
handful sesame seeds for decoration

PASTRY
250 g (8 oz) self-raising flour
pinch of salt
4 oz margarine
cold water, to mix

Stir-Fried Rice

Heat the oil in a pan, add ginger and cabbage and saute until slightly brown. Add water, orange rind, sultanas or raisins, orange juice, lemon juice, salt and pepper. Bring to boil and simmer for 15 minutes. Drain the rice, add to the pan and cook until the rice is tender and all the water is absorbed. Reduce the heat to the lowest mark, cover the pan and allow it to cook further for 2-3 minutes.

Serve garnished with mint or coriander leaves.

SERVES 4-5.

3 tbs oil
1 tsp fresh ginger, finely grated
125 g (4 oz) white cabbage, finely shredded
900 ml (1½ pints) water
rind of ½ orange, grated
60 g (2 oz) sultanas OR raisins
1 tbs orange juice
1 tbs lemon juice
salt and pepper, to taste
250 g (8 oz) white rice, soaked
handful of fresh mint OR coriander leaves, chopped

Stuffed Aubergines

Set the oven to 190°C/375°F/Gas Mark 5. Cut the aubergines in half lenghtways and place the cut side upwards on a greased baking sheet. Brush the cut sides with oil and bake for 20 minutes. Heat the oil in a pan and stir-fry the celery gently for 2-3 minutes. Add the mushrooms and cook, stirring for 3 minutes.

Stir in rice, walnuts, tomato purée, parsley and seasoning. Scoop the flesh from the aubergines, without breaking the skins. Chop the flesh finely and mix with the fried mixture. Pile back into the aubergine skins, sprinkle with cheese and place under a hot grill until cheese has melted.

Serve immediately with a salad.

SERVES 4.

2 large aubergines (eggplant)
2-3 tbs oil
3 sticks celery, finely chopped
210 g (7 oz) mushrooms, thinly sliced
6 tbs rice, cooked
60 g (2 oz) walnuts, coarsely chopped
1 tsp tomato purée
2 tbs fresh parsley, chopped
salt and pepper, to taste
75 g (2½ oz) Cheddar cheese, grated

Stuffed Cabbage

Boil the cabbage leaves for 5 minutes in salted water. Keep the water (stock) and put the cabbage aside to drain. Mix the remaining ingredients together and form into 6 balls. Wrap each ball with a cabbage leaf, secure with a cocktail stick and place in an ovenproof dish. Cover with a little of the cabbage stock.

Bake in the oven at 200°C/400°F/Gas Mark 6 for 30-40 minutes.

Adding a little cornflour can thicken the stock.

SERVES 6.

6 large Savoy cabbage leaves
125 g (4 oz) brown rice, cooked
60 g (2 oz) mushrooms, chopped
125 g (4 oz) soya mince
salt and pepper, to taste
2 tsp oil

Vegetable Rolls

Steam all the vegetables together until just soft, and mash.

Melt the butter or margarine in a saucepan. Add flour and then gradually add the milk to make a smooth white sauce.

Mix the sauce with the mashed vegetables. Add cheese and oatmeal to make a firm dough. Shape the dough into oval shaped rolls. Deep fry in hot oil, turning constantly until golden brown all over.

Serve with a salad.

SERVES 6.

1 small cauliflower, small florets
2 carrots, cubed
2 potatoes, cubed
125 g (4 oz) courgettes (zucchini), cubed
125 g (4 oz) green peas
60 g (2 oz) butter OR margarine
60 g (2 oz) flour
250 ml (8 fl oz) milk
125 g (4 oz) mild Cheddar cheese, grated
125 g (4 oz) oatmeal
oil, for deep frying

Stir-Fried Vegetables (Opposite)

Heat oil in a wok and stir-fry each vegetable individually for 2-3 minutes adding ginger to one of them.

Stir-fry tofu over medium heat in a flat wok until both sides slightly brown and add to the stir-fried vegetables. Stir in soya sauce and sesame oil.

Serve with noodles or rice.

SERVES 6.

3 tbs oil
2 tbs fresh ginger – grated finely
125 g (4 oz) broccoli, broken into florets
125 g (4 oz) cauliflower, broken into florets
250 g (8 oz) baby sweetcorn, cut in two diagonally
125 g (4 oz) mangetout cut into strips
125 g (4 oz) carrots, cut into matchsticks
125 g (4 oz) mushrooms, sliced
2 red peppers, cut into strips
2 green peppers, cut into strips
125 g (4 oz) hard tofu, cut into sticks
soya sauce, to taste
1 tsp sesame oil
pepper, to taste

Vegetable Flans

To make pastry, put the flours and margarine into a mixing bowl and rub lightly together with fingertips until the mixture resembles breadcrumbs. Add enough water to make a firm dough. Roll out the pastry on a lightly floured surface and line six 14 cm (5 ½ in) individual flan tins. Prick the base of each flan and chill for ½ hour. Line each flan with greaseproof paper or aluminium foil and fill with dried beans. Bake blind in a hot oven at 200°C/400°F/Gas Mark 6 for 10 minutes. Remove the beans and paper or foil. Keep the beans to use again.

Heat the oil, gently fry the vegetables, add herbs and seasoning, then cook for 2-3 minutes. Spoon the mixture into the flan cases. Beat the yoghurt, cornflour and milk together, add the cream and cheese; mix well and pour over the filling.

Bake the flans at 190°C/375°F/Gas Mark 5 for 15-20 minutes or until set.

MAKES 6 FLANS.

PASTRY
300 g (10 oz) wholewheat flour
180 g (6 oz) plain flour
250 g (8 oz) margarine
cold water, to mix
dried beans, for baking blind

FILLING
1 tbs oil
1 red pepper, sliced
180 g (6 oz) courgettes (zucchini), thinly sliced
4 tomatoes, skinned and chopped
1 tbs fresh marjoram, chopped
1 tbs fresh basil, chopped
salt and pepper, to taste
1 tbs plain yoghurt
1 tbs cornflour
1 tbs milk
100 ml (3 fl oz) single cream
60 g (2 oz) Cheddar cheese, grated

Stuffed Peppers (Opposite)

Slice off the top of the pepper and discard the seeds. Fry the soya mince in oil; add hot water and allow it stand for 10 minutes. Combine the soya mince, rice, salt, pepper, sesame oil, soya sauce and coriander leaves. Fill each pepper with this mixture.

Place the peppers on a baking tray, sprinkle cheese on top and bake at 325°F/160°C/Gas Mark 3 for 20-30 minutes.

Serve with salad.

SERVES 3.

3 peppers (green, red or yellow)
60 g (2 oz) soya mince
2-3 tbs hot water
1 tbs oil
125 g (4 oz) brown rice, cooked
salt and pepper, to taste
½ tsp sesame oil
2 tbs soya sauce
60 g (2 oz) fresh coriander leaves
125 g (4 oz) Cheddar cheese, grated

Vegetable Pancakes

Whisk together self-raising flour, milk, salt and pepper until the batter becomes smooth and creamy. Leave to stand for 5 minutes, then add all the ingredients except the oil.

Heat 1 tablespoon of oil in a frying pan, spread the pancake mixture evenly over the pan and allow it to cook on a low heat until golden, then turn it over to cook the other side. A few drops of oil can be added to the side of the pan to prevent sticking.

Serve hot.

MAKES 6-8.

250 g (8 oz) self-raising flour
milk, to mix
salt and pepper, to taste
60 g (2 oz) cabbage, finely shredded
60 g (2 oz) frozen corn
2 medium-sized tomatoes, diced
1 green pepper, diced small
1 tsp ginger, grated finely
herbs, of your choice
oil, for frying

Tagliatelle with Mushrooms (Opposite)

Fill a large saucepan ¾ full with water, add salt and few drops of oil, bring to the boil, add tagliatelle and cook until just tender. Meanwhile, fry the mushrooms in butter and add salt and pepper. Drain the tagliatelle and place in a bowl, mix in the cheese, double cream and fried mushrooms. Sprinkle with parsley and serve immediately.

Optional: add basil and paprika to the cream.

SERVES 4-5.

500 g (1 lb) tagliatelle
250 g (8 oz) mushrooms, chopped
2 tsp butter
salt and pepper, to taste
90 g (3 oz) Cheddar cheese, grated
250 ml (8 fl oz) double cream
2 tbs fresh parsley, chopped

Vegetable Pie

Peel the potatoes and cut the large ones in half. Cover with cold water and 2 teaspoons of salt, bring to the boil and cook for 20-25 minutes, then drain and slice into ¼ inch. Melt 60 g (2 oz) of butter or margarine in a medium sized saucepan and sauté the carrots. Add Brussels sprouts and 3 tablespoons water.

Cover and cook gently for 2 minutes, stirring occasionally. Stir in the sage, salt and pepper. Stir in the flour, and cook over a low heat for 2 minutes. Gradually stir in the milk and cook for 3 minutes or until thickened. Remove the pan from the heat.

Arrange half the potatoes on the base of an ovenproof dish, and cover with the sprout and carrot mixture. Arrange the remainder of the potatoes over the top. Melt the remaining butter or margarine and brush over the potatoes. Spread the cheese on top. Grill gently until brown.

SERVES 4-6.

1 kg (2 lb) potatoes
2 tsp salt
90 g (3 oz) butter OR margarine
375 g (12 oz) carrots, sliced round
375 g (12 oz) Brussels sprouts, halved
3 tbs water
¼ tsp dried sage
salt and pepper, to taste
30 g (1 oz) flour
150 ml (¼ pint) milk
90 g (3 oz) mild Cheddar cheese, grated
    for topping

Tofu Flan

Stir-fry the vegetables in the oil for 5 minutes, then set aside. Mix the tofu with the fried vegetables, walnuts, salt, vinegar and herbs.

Sift the flour and salt, make a well in the middle for the oil. Rub the oil lightly into the flour until the mixture resembles breadcrumbs. Add a little water; mix together, then press into a 12 in flan tin. Cover with tofu mixture, decorate with tomato and bake at 200°C/400°F/Gas Mark 6 for 25-30 minutes.

SERVES 4-5.

FILLING
1 large carrot, diced
420 g (14 oz) broccoli, chopped
2 - 3 tbs oil
375 g (¾ lb) tofu, drained and mashed
60 g (2 oz) walnuts, chopped
1½ tsp salt
5 tsp cider vinegar
1 tsp herbs (optional)
1 large tomato, sliced for decorating

PASTRY
625 g (1¼ lb) plain flour
pinch of salt
270 ml (9 fl oz) oil
cold water, to mix

Vegetable Rice

Rinse and drain the rice. Heat 1 teaspoon of the oil in a pan, add the rice and cook for 2 minutes, stirring continuously on a low heat. Add hot water and bring to the boil. Reduce the heat and simmer for 40-45 minutes, adding more water if necessary.

Heat the remaining oil in another pan, add red pepper and mushrooms and fry for 3 minutes. Stir in the cooked rice and flaked almonds, adjust seasoning to taste and sprinkle with parsley and cheese.

SERVES 3-4.

250 g (8 oz) brown rice
3 tsp oil
600 ml (1 pint) hot water
1 red pepper, chopped
420 g (14 oz) mushrooms, quartered
60 g (2 oz) almonds, flaked
salt and pepper, to taste
1 tbs parsley
90 g (3 oz) Cheddar cheese, grated for
*   topping*

Vegetarian Shepherd's Pie

Peel the potatoes. Put them in a saucepan, cover with boiling water, cover and boil until just soft. Meanwhile to prepare the filling, heat 2 tablespoons of oil in a wok or frying pan, add asafoetida and cabbage and stir-fry until slightly brown. Then add carrots, mushrooms and sweetcorn. Stir-fry together for 5 more minutes. Fry the soya mince separately in 2 tablespoons of oil for 5 minutes and then add to the filling. Make a tomato sauce separately with the blended tomatoes and 1 tablespoon of oil. Simmer the filling for 5 minutes and add mixed herbs, salt, pepper and parsley. Add the tomato sauce to the filling and mix well. Add more salt and pepper if necessary.

Drain and mash the potatoes. Add butter, milk, a handful of the grated cheese, parsley, salt and pepper and mix until creamy. Spread the mashed potatoes over the filling. Sprinkle with the remaining cheese and bake in the oven at 200°C/400°F/Gas Mark 6 for 20 minutes until golden brown.

SERVES 3-4.

500 g (1 lb) potatoes
60 g (2 oz) butter
180 ml (6 fl oz) milk
125 g (4 oz) mild Cheddar cheese, grated
fresh parsley, chopped
salt and pepper, to taste

FILLING
5 tbs vegetable oil
½ tsp asafoetida (hing)
125 g (4 oz) cabbage
250 g (8 oz) grated carrots
500 g (1 lb) chopped mushrooms
250 g (8 oz) canned or frozen sweetcorn
250 g (8 oz) soya mince
220 g (7 oz) canned tomatoes, blended
1 tsp mixed herbs
salt and pepper, to taste
fresh parsley, chopped

Walnut Cheese Burgers

Fry the mushrooms and cabbage in a tablespoon of oil or butter. Mix all the ingredients together to form into a firm mixture. Add a little milk if needed. Shape into balls and flatten into burger shapes. Fry in oil in a shallow pan until brown on both sides.

Serve with Tomato Sauce (page 89) and a salad.

MAKES 6-8 BURGERS.

60 g (2 oz) mushrooms, finely chopped
60 g (2 oz) cabbage, shredded
1 tbs oil OR butter
180 g (6 oz) walnuts, ground
60 g (2 oz) breadcrumbs
125 g (4 oz) cheese
salt and pepper, to taste
1 tbs tomato purée
handful of fresh parsley, chopped
2 tbs milk
60 g (2 oz) soya mince
oil, for frying

Sauces & Chutneys

Brown Gravy

Mix water, soya sauce and cornflour in a saucepan. Stir until the cornflour dissolves. Place over a low heat and stir continuously until the the gravy thickens. Add herbs, salt and pepper.

Serve on stir-fried vegetables.

125 ml (4 fl oz) water
60 ml (2 fl oz) dark soya sauce
2-3 tbs cornflour
1 tsb mixed herbs
Salt and pepper to taste

Cashew Gravy

Blend all ingredients in a blender, then heat in a saucepan, stirring with a wooden spoon until thick and almost boiling.

Serve on pies or vegetables.

180g (6oz) cashew nuts, ground
600ml (1 pints) milk OR water
5 tsp arrowroot
1 tsp celery seed, ground
1 tsp asafoetida (hing)
2 tbs olive oil
1 tsp salt

Mushroom Gravy

Sauté mushrooms in butter or oil in a pan. Mix water, cornflour, and soya sauce until the cornflour dissolves and add gradually to the mushrooms, stirring constantly. Bring to the boil until it thickens. Simmer for 3-4 minutes. Add pepper.

Serve with mashed potatoes or steamed, boiled or stir-fried vegetables.

60 g (2 oz) mushrooms, sliced
1 tbs butter OR oil
2 tbs cornflour
250 ml (8 fl oz) water
2 tbs soya sauce
pepper, to taste

Yoghurt Mint Sauce

Mix all the ingredients together and serve.

125 ml (4 fl oz) plain yoghurt
2 tbs mint, chopped
1 small green chilli, de-seeded and finely chopped
salt, to taste

Sweet and Sour Sauce

Stir all the ingredients together over a medium heat until the sauce boils and thickens.

3 tbs cider vinegar
3 tbs tomato purée
250 ml (8 fl oz) water
4-5 tbs sugar
pinch of asafoetida (hing)
2 tbs cornflour

Tomato Sauce

Heat the oil in a small pan with a pinch of asafoetida. Add the tomato purée, water, lemon juice and cornflour. Keep stirring until the sauce thickens. Add the sugar, salt and pepper.

Serve on chips and burgers or any savoury dishes.

1 tbs oil
pinch of asafoetida (hing)
2-3 tbs tomato purée
250 ml (8 fl oz) water
2-3 tbs lemon juice
1-2 tbs cornflour
1 tbs sugar
salt and pepper, to taste

White Sauce

Melt the butter or margarine in a saucepan and add the flour. Cook for 2-3 minutes, stirring well with a whisk or wooden spoon. Add the water and the milk. Stir continuously to ensure that there are no lumps. Cook until the sauce thickens to a smooth and even consistency. Season with salt, pepper and nutmeg. For a thinner sauce, add more liquid.

OR If using cornflour, mix all the ingredients in a saucepan and bring to boil over medium heat. Stir continuously until the sauce thinkens.

30 g (1 oz) butter OR margarine
30 g (1 oz) plain flour OR cornflour
150 ml (¼ pint) water
300 ml (½ pint) milk
salt and pepper, to taste
pinch of nutmeg, ground

Variations:
1. **White Sauce**: adding 90 g (3 oz) grated cheese after the sauce is cooked. Mild, mature or strong Cheddar can be used, depending upon taste.
2. **Parsley Sauce**: as White Sauce, adding 30 g (1 oz) chopped fresh parsley.

Chutney for Pakoras

Place all the ingredients in a blender and blend to make into a chutney.

1 small carrot, chopped
1 cucumber, cut small pieces
3 medium tomatoes - chopped
3 green chillies chopped
1 small raw mango-grated coarsely OR
     juice of ½ lemon
2 tsp cumin seeds
salt and sugar, to taste
2 tbs fresh coriander leaves

Green Chilli Chutney

Place everything in a blender and blend thoroughly.

bunch of coriander leaves OR parsley,
     washed and chopped
2-3 green chillies, chopped
½ apple, peeled and cubed
¼ tsp sugar
juice of ½ lemon
1 level tsp salt

Red Pepper Chutney

Remove the seeds from the red pepper and chop coarsely. Blend all the ingredients together, except the coriander leaves. Garnish with chopped coriander leaves.

1 red pepper
3 green chillies
2 tsp cumin seeds
juice of ½ lemon
salt, to taste
sugar, to taste
1 tbs coriander leaves, chopped

Red Plum Chutney

Put plums and apples into a large saucepan, add the remaining ingredients. Bring slowly to the boil, stirring continuously, until the sugar has dissolved. Lower the heat and simmer, stirring in between to prevent sticking and burning uncovered, until the chutney is thick and mushy - about 30 minutes. Store in jar.

1 kg (2 lb) red plums, halved and stoned
500 g (1 lb) cooking apples, peeled, cored and chopped
500 g (1 lb) demerara sugar
2 tsp ginger, grated
1 tsp mixed spice
600 ml (1 pint) pickling vinegar

Tomato Chutney

Place the whole tomatoes in hot boiling water and boil for 1 minute, the skin will begin to split. Remove the tomatoes from the water and leave to cool before peeling off the skin.

Place tomatoes in a pan, add peeled and sliced apples with vinegar, sugar, cayenne, cloves and cinnamon. Bring to boil and simmer, stirring occasionally until the sugar has dissolved and the fruit and vegetables are tender. Pour into warmed, dry jars and add one or two green chillies to each jar. Allow to cool, cover tightly and store.

500 g (1 lb) fresh tomatoes
1 tbs salt
3 large Bramley apples
300 ml (½ pint) cider vinegar
500 g (1 lb) sugar
1 tsp cayenne pepper
1 tsp cloves, ground
1 tsp cinnamon, ground
green chillies (optional)

Side Dishes

Baked Beans (Opposite)

Drain and rinse the soaked beans. Cook for 1 hour in plenty of water until soft and tender or pressure cook for 15 minutes. Meanwhile, blend tomatoes and purée together. Heat the oil in a pan and add blended tomatoes. Add salt, pepper, vinegar and sugar and simmer for 10-15 minutes. Add the beans to the sauce and simmer for a further 10 minutes.

SERVES 10.

500 g (1 lb) haricot beans, soaked overnight
400 g (14 oz) canned tomatoes
3 tsp tomato purée
2 tbs oil
salt and pepper, to taste
1 tsb vinegar, malt or cider
1 tbs sugar

Green Beans with Flaked Almonds

Cook the beans in boiling water until tender. Melt half the butter or margarine in a frying pan. Add almonds and fry until golden brown, then remove from the pan. Melt the remaining butter or margarine and stir-fry the beans for 1 minute. Add salt and pepper. Place in a serving dish and sprinkle with fried almonds.

Serve with mashed potato.

SERVES 4.

500 g (1 lb) French beans cut to 1 inch pieces
60 g (2 oz) butter OR margarine
125 g (4 oz) almonds, flaked
salt and pepper, to taste

Broccoli with Ginger Sauce

Heat the oil and a little of the ginger in a wok or frying pan until hot. Stir-fry broccoli for 2-3 minutes or until tender. Combine soya sauce, water, cornflour and the remaining ginger and pour over the broccoli, tossing and turning the broccoli until the sauce thickens.

SERVES 4-6.

1 tbs oil
1 tbs fresh ginger, grated finely
1 large broccoli, broken into small florets

SAUCE
2 tbs light soya sauce
125 ml (4 fl oz) water
2 tbs cornflour

Broccoli with Walnuts

Heat 2 tablespoons oil in a frying pan and stir-fry the the broccoli for 2-3minutes until crisp and tender. Then stir-fry the mushrooms separately in 2 tablespoons of oil for 2-3 minutes and add to the broccoli. Add walnuts, salt, pepper and mint and stir for 1 minute.

SERVES 4-5.

1 large broccoli, broken into small florets
4 tbs olive oil
60 g (2 oz) mushrooms, quartered
60 g (2 oz) walnuts, chopped
salt and pepper, to taste
1 tsp mint

Dhokra (Opposite)

For this recipe you will need a wok with a lid.

Mix all the batter ingredients (except the Eno) in a big bowl, adding enough warm water to make a thick batter (like pancake batter). Leave aside for 10-15 minutes. Quarter fill a wok with water and bring to the boil.

Lightly oil a round 8in tray. Mix the Eno's into the batter, beat it thoroughly and pour it into the oiled tray. Place the tray in the wok of boiling water, cover and steam for 15 minutes. Make sure the water remains below the tray and the wok doesn't boil dry.

Note: to test if the dhokra are ready, put a clean knife in the centre of the tray, it should come out clean. They should be light and spongy.

Remove the tray from the wok (taking care not to get burnt). Allow to cool and cut into squares.

For the topping, heat oil in a saucepan. Add the mustard and sesame seeds and cover with a lid. Once the seeds have popped, remove from the heat and spread over the dhokra with a spoon. Sprinkle freshly chopped coriander leaves, coconut and chillies as desired and serve.

MAKES 1 TRAY.

FOR THE BATTER
180g (6oz) gram flour (chickpeas flour)
30g (1oz) rice flour
180ml (6fl oz) plain yoghurt
1 tsp salt
2 tsp sugar (optional)
¼ tsp level citric acid
3 desert spoons cooking oil
60-70 mls (2.5 fl oz) warm water
(enough to form into thick batter)
1 heap tsp Eno's fruit salts

TOPPING
2 tbs cooking oil
1 tsp mustard seeds
1 tsp sesame seeds (optional)
1 tbs desicatted coconut
1 green chilli finely chopped (optional)
1 tbs fresh coriander leaves, chopped

Brussels Sprouts au Gratin

Discard the outer leaves and wash the Brussels sprouts thoroughly. Steam for 5 to 7 minutes then place in a greased 25 x 30 cm (10 x 12 in) ovenproof dish. Cover with Cheese Sauce. Sprinkle the top with grated cheese and breadcrumbs.

Bake at 180°C/350°F/Gas Mark 4 for 20-25 minutes.

SERVES 6.

500g (1 lb) Brussels sprouts
Cheese Sauce (page 89)
30 g (1 oz) Cheddar cheese, grated
60 g (2 oz) breadcrumbs

Peperonata (Opposite)

Wash and dry the peppers and aubergine. Slice the peppers from top to bottom, remove the stem and seeds and slice into long fingers. Slice the aubergine from top to bottom, cut the slices in half width ways and then lengthways into fingers. Heat the oil in a frying pan or wok. Add the peppers and aubergine and cook on a low heat for 5 minutes. Add the chopped tomatoes and chilli. Cook for a further 25 minutes stirring frequently. Add salt and pepper to taste. Garnish with chopped parsley or coriander leaves.

Serve with Pitta Bread.

SERVES 4.

8 peppers (2 red, 2 orange, 2 yellow and
2 green, or whatever is available)
1 aubergine (eggplant)
2 tbs olive oil OR sunflower oil
4 fresh tomatoes, chopped
1 fresh green chilli or red chilli, chopped
(optional)
salt and pepper, to taste
parsley OR coriander leaves, chopped

Hungarian Courgettes

Melt half the butter or margarine in a saucepan, stir in the courgettes, cook until soft and slightly transparent and place in large bowl. Melt the remaining butter or margarine, add the mushrooms and stir-fry for 2-3 minutes. Mix all the ingredients, except the cheese and almond flakes, together in a large bowl. Transfer to an oven dish and bake at 160°C/325°F/Gas Mark 3 until crisp. Cover with the cheese and bake for a further 10 minutes. Sprinkle flaked almonds, before serving.

SERVES 4.

25 ml (4 oz) butter OR margarine
500 g (1 lb) courgettes (zucchini), sliced
250 g (8 oz) mushrooms, sliced
90 g (3 oz) fresh breadcrumbs
150 ml (¼ pint) sour cream
60 g (2 oz) almonds, flaked
1 tsp paprika
60 g (2 oz) Cheddar cheese, grated

Chick Pea and Coriander Patties

Drain and rinse the chick peas and blend them with oil in a food processor until smooth. Mix in the spices, coriander leaves and parsley. Stir in the flour, salt and pepper and leave for 15 minutes. Roll the mixture into 12 balls, the size of golf balls. Flatten into patties and deep fry in oil until golden.

Serve with Yoghurt (page 212) and Tomato Sauce (page 89).

MAKES 12 PATTIES.

500 g (1 lb) chick peas, soaked overnight
1 tbs oil
2 tsp cumin seeds, ground
2 tsp coriander seeds, ground
½ tsp chilli, ground (optional)
2 tsp coriander leaves, chopped
1 tbs parsley, chopped
2 tbs plain flour
salt and pepper, to taste
oil, for frying

Quick Pilau Rice (Opposite)

Wash the rice. Heat the oil in a pan, add mustard seeds, cumin seeds and asafoetida. Fry until the seeds pop. Add the frozen vegetables, raisins, salt and ginger and cook for 2 minutes. Add the water and stir in the rice. Bring to boil, reduce the heat. Cover the pan and cook on a low heat for about 20 minutes.

SERVES 3-4.

125 g (4 oz) rice
2 tbs oil
¼ tsp mustard seeds
¼ tsp cumin seeds
pinch of asafoetida (hing)
60 g (2 oz) frozen mixed vegetables
1 tsp salt
1 tbs fresh ginger, finely grated
450 ml (¾ pint) water
handful raisins

Jamaican Rice

Drain and rinse the red kidney beans. Pressure cook them until soft and drain them. Mix with rice, coconut cream, salt, mixed herbs or Jamaican thyme, asafoetida and chillies. Best served with salad.

Variation: If a pressure cooker is not available, cook the beans until tender. Substitute red kidney beans with adzuki beans or black-eyed beans.

SERVES 4-6.

180 g (6 oz) red kidney beans (soaked for 1 hour in hot water OR in cold water overnight)
250 g (8 oz) rice, cooked
60 ml (2 fl oz) coconut cream
salt, to taste
2 tsp mixed herbs OR Jamaican thyme
¼ tsp asafoetida (hing)
green chillies (optional)

Crunchy Cabbage

Discard the excess stalk and wash the cabbage thoroughly; then shred it. Bring the water and salt to the boil in a large saucepan and add the shredded cabbage. Cover and cook for 2-3 minutes. Drain well, place in a baking dish.

Melt the butter or margarine in a saucepan, add peanuts, breadcrumbs and cheese and mix well. Spread over the cabbage and bake at 190°C/375°F/Gas Mark 5 for 10 minutes.

SERVES 4-5.

750 g (1½ lb) white cabbage
300 ml (½ pint) water
1 tsp salt
60 g (2 oz) butter OR margarine
60 g (2 oz) salted peanuts
30 g (1 oz) breadcrumbs
30 g (1 oz) mild Cheddar cheese, grated

Potato Pancakes (Opposite)

Wash, peel and coarsely grate the potatoes. Add salt, pepper and spices. Heat 1 tablespoon of butter, margarine or oil in a heavy-based frying pan. Put in 1½ tablespoonful of potatoes, pressing evenly over the pan with a spoon. Cook, uncovered, over a medium heat until brown both sides. Turn the potato pancake over. You can add a little more butter, margarine or oil to the pan if required.

SERVES 7.

7 potatoes
salt and pepper, to taste
1 tsp mixed spices
butter OR margarine OR oil

Mushroom and Tomato Sauce

Heat the oil in a pan and cook the tomatoes for 5 minutes. Add the mushrooms, mint, salt and pepper. Cover and cook further for 5-10 minutes.

Serve with croutons or toast.

SERVES 2.

2 tbs oil
2 large tomatoes, peeled and chopped
250 g (8 oz) mushrooms, sliced
1 tsp mint, chopped
salt and pepper, to taste

Fried Aubergine

Cut the aubergine into 1 cm (½ in) thick slices. Heat the butter or oil in a pan. Fry aubergine slices for about 2-3 minute each side, turning 3 or 4 times if necessary. Fry until crisp on the outside and tender inside. Turn onto a plate and sprinkle with salt, pepper and basil.

SERVES 3.

1 large aubergine (eggplant)
2 tbs butter OR oil
salt and pepper, to taste
1 tsp basil

Roast Potatoes (Opposite)

Par-boil the potatoes in salt water for 10 minutes. Drain and place on a lightly greased baking tray. Sprinkle with dried rosemary or oregano, oil and peppercorns. Make sure the potatoes are well covered with oil before baking. Bake in a hot oven at 200°C/400°F/Gas Mark 6 for 40-50 minutes until golden brown, turning occasionally.

SERVES 4-5.

500 g (1 lb) potatoes, peeled and quartered
boiling water, with a pinch of salt
1 tsp dried rosemary OR oregano
125 ml (4 fl oz) oil
a few crushed peppercorns

Lentil Rolls

Heat 3 tablespoons oil in a pan and gently fry celery, carrots and cabbage for 2-4 minutes. Add lentils, water and seasoning. Bring to the boil, cover and simmer for 50-60 minutes until the water is absorbed, stirring occasionally. Mix in the parsley and a third of the breadcrumbs. Leave to cool. Using floured hands, shape the mixture into cylindrical rolls and coat with the flour. Dip each roll into the milk and coat with the remaining breadcrumbs. Pour oil into a frying pan to a depth of 5 mm (¼ in) and place over a moderate heat. When hot, add the rolls and fry until crisp and golden brown, turning once or twice.

Serve with Yoghurt (page 212) and Cucumber Raita (page 40).

MAKES 10 ROLLS.

3 tbs oil
2 sticks celery, finely chopped
2 carrots, peeled and grated
60 g (2 oz) cabbage, finely shredded
270 g (9 oz) yellow lentils
600 ml (1 pint) water
salt and pepper, to taste
2 tbs fresh parsley, chopped
180 g (6 oz) wholemeal breadcrumbs
2 tbs flour
milk for coating
oil, for deep frying

Fried Rice

Put the cooked rice into a saucepan or bowl. Wash and cook the mushrooms in a little boiling water until tender, then drain. The water can be reserved for soup or stock. Chop the mushrooms into small pieces, discarding the hard stems. Cut the tofu into small cubes and fry in a little oil until brown. Stir-fry the carrots separately in a little oil for 4-5 minutes and add to the rice. Put more oil in the wok and stir-fry the remaining vegetables for 3-4 minutes, adding soya sauce and pepper to taste. Gently mix all the vegetables with the rice, finally adding the fried tofu. Sprinkle with sesame oil and serve.

SERVES 4-6.

500 g (1 lb) brown or white rice, cooked
125 ml (4 oz) dried Chinese mushrooms
125 g (4 oz) firm tofu
3-4 tbs oil
2 carrots, diced
60 g (2 oz) sweetcorn, frozen
1 dried or fresh green pepper
1 dried or fresh red pepper
soya sauce
black pepper to taste
1 tbs sesame oil

Roast Parsnips (Opposite)

Cut the parsnips into 4 lengthways and place on a baking tray. Pour oil over the parsnips, making sure they are well oiled. Sprinkle with salt and peppercorns and bake in hot oven at 200°C/400°F/Gas Mark 6 for 30 minutes or until golden-brown.

SERVES 4.

500 g (1 lb) parsnips, peeled
60 ml (2 fl oz) oil
pinch of salt
1 tbs peppercorns

Savoury Rice

Heat 2-3 tablespoons of oil in a wok and add ginger. Fry for 30 seconds, then add all the vegetables and stir-fry until tender. Add the cooked rice, salt, pepper, parsley or coriander and sesame oil and mix gently.

Serve hot.

SERVES 4-5.

3 tbs oil
30 g (1 oz) fresh ginger, finely grated
60 g (2 oz) carrots, diced
60 g (2 oz) mushrooms, chopped
1 green pepper, chopped
60 g (2 oz) frozen corn
250 g (8 oz) rice cooked (white or brown)
salt and pepper, to taste
a handful of chopped fresh parsley OR
    coriander leaves
1 tsp sesame oil

Fried Rice Balls

Wash the rice and place in a saucepan with water and 1 teaspoon of salt. Bring to the boil, cover and simmer until tender.

Blend the flour with 2 teaspoons of salt, pepper and enough water to make a thick batter. In a separate bowl, blend milk, yoghurt and cornflour, and add to the rice. Add paprika or chillies, basil, cheese and mashed potato to the rice and mix until firm. Roll spoonfuls of mixture into walnut sized balls, dip into the batter until fully covered and deep fry in fairly hot oil until golden brown.

Serve hot with Tomato Sauce (page 89).

MAKES 10-12 BALLS.

250 g (8 oz) brown rice
600 ml (1 pint) water
3 level tsp salt
270 g (9 oz) plain flour
1 tsp pepper
1 tbs milk
1 tbs yoghurt
1 tbs cornflour
1 tsp paprika OR 1-2 fresh chillies, chopped
handful of fresh basil, chopped
155 g (5 oz) Cheddar cheese, grated
2 medium-sized potatoes, cooked and mashed
oil, for deep frying

Savoury Vermicelli (Opposite)

Heat the oil in a large pan. Add cumin seeds and sauté for a few seconds. Then add all the vegetables. Stir in the salt, green chilli, turmeric, ground coriander and garam masala. When the vegetables are nearly cooked, add lemon juice to taste.

Half fill a medium sized pan with water and add 1 teaspoon of oil and ½ teaspoon of salt. Bring to the boil. Add the vermicelli and cook for 2-3 minutes. Drain in a sieve and rinse under cold water.

Mix the vermicelli with the vegetables and cook for a few more minutes. Add fresh coriander leaves to garnish. Serve hot.

SERVES 6.

2 tbs oil
½ tsp cumin seeds
2 potatoes, finely chopped
2 carrots, finely chopped
1 green pepper, finely chopped
60 g (2 oz) corn and 60 g (2 oz) peas OR
125 g (4 oz) mixed vegetables
3 fresh tomatoes, chopped
1 green chilli, chopped
½ tsp turmeric, powder
1 tsp coriander seeds, ground
1 tsp garam masala
lemon juice
1 tsp oil
½ tsp salt
250 g (8 oz) vermicelli
salt to taste
fresh coriander leaves, finely chopped

Green Beans in Tomato

Put all the ingredients into a saucepan. Bring to boil, stirring constantly. Lower the heat and simmer for about 5 minutes until the beans are tender. Stir from time to time to prevent sticking.

Serve with bread or Pitta Bread.

SERVES 4-5.

500 g (1 lb) fresh or frozen runner beans, if using fresh beans, cut into 1-2 inch pieces
6 tbs tomato purée
4 tbs olive oil
250 ml (8 fl oz) water
salt and pepper, to taste
1 tsp oregano

Saffron Rice

Dissolve the saffron in hot water. Put the rice into a saucepan with cold water, salt and the saffron water. Bring to the boil, cover and simmer until cooked and all the water is absorbed. Sprinkle with almonds.

SERVES 3-4.

12 saffron threads
2 tbs hot water
250 g (8 oz) white rice, washed
500 ml (16 fl oz) cold water
1 tsp salt
1 tbs almonds, flaked

Stuffed Mushrooms (Opposite)

Set the oven to 180°C/350°F/Gas Mark 4. Wash and remove the stalks from the mushrooms. Place with the rounded side down in an oiled ovenproof dish. Chop the mushroom stalks and stir-fry in butter for 1-2 minutes; add parsley, cream, breadcrumbs and season and mix. Place a spoonful of this mixture in each mushroom cap.

Sprinkle cheese and bake for 20 minutes until golden.

Sprinkle with thyme and serve hot.

SERVES 4.

6 large mushrooms
2 tbs oil
1 tbs fresh parsley, chopped
2 tbs cream
60 g (2 oz) breadcrumbs
salt and pepper, to taste
30 g (1 oz) butter OR margarine
60 g (2 oz) mild Cheddar cheese, grated
½ tsp fresh thyme, chopped

Okra with Tomatoes

Wash okra and pat dry on paper towel; top and tail. Cut the peppers lengthways and remove the seeds. Chop into strips. Chop the red chilli very finely. Heat the oil in a large saucepan and add the okra. Cook for 5-7 minutes over a medium heat tossing from time to time. Add green pepper, chilli, tomatoes, salt and pepper to the pan. Cover and cook on low heat for a further 10 minutes, stirring occasionally, until the okra is tender. Sprinkle with chopped coriander leaves.

Serve with Yoghurt (page 212) OR Cucumber Raita (page 40).

SERVES 4-5.

500 g (1 lb) small okra
1 small green pepper
1 small red chilli
3 large tomatoes, chopped
3 tbs oil
salt and pepper, to taste
handful of coriander leaves, chopped

Paneer in Green Masala

Bring the milk to the boil, add the yoghurt or lemon juice. The milk should start to curdle add more yoghurt if necessary and the paneer should separate from the water. Strain into a muslin cloth, pat it flat, fold the muslin cloth over and place it under a heavy weight for 1-2 hours, to allow the water to drain out completely and for the paneer to set. When set, cut into 1 cm (½ in) cubes and keep aside.

Liquidise the tomatoes, coriander leaves, ginger and green chilli together. Add a little salt to retain the green colour.

Heat oil in a frying pan, add the cumin seeds and curry leaves until the seeds start sizzling. Add the turmeric, garam masala and liquidised ingredients. Simmer for 15 minutes, gently stir in the paneer and add salt to taste. Simmer for another 5 minutes or longer until the gravy thickens.

Serve with rice or Chapatis (page 179).

SERVES 4.

PANEER
2.4 l (4 pints) full cream milk
275 ml (½ pint) plain yoghurt OR
   juice of 3 lemons

GRAVY
3-4 fresh tomatoes
½ bunch of coriander, finely chopped
   (about a cupful)
1 tbs ginger, grated finely
1 green chilli
   (optional for an extra hot dish)
salt
1 tsp cumin seeds
8-10 curry leaves
1 tbs oil
½ tsp turmeric, powder
½ tsp garam masala

Pasta with Herbs

Fill a large saucepan ¾ full with water, bring to the boil, then add pasta spirals and cook until just tender. Drain well.

Liquidise all the other ingredients, except the cucumber, in a blender for 2-3 minutes. Add to the pasta and mix in the cucumber.

Cool in the refrigerator before serving.

SERVES 3-4.

300 g (10 oz) pasta spirals
30 g (1 oz) fresh mixed herbs
2 tbs apple juice
1 tbs plain yoghurt
¼ tsp dijon mustard
2 tbs olive oil
salt and pepper, to taste
1 cucumber, sliced in half circle

Potato Balls (Aloo Vada)

Heat 2 tablespoons of oil in a saucepan, add the mustard seeds and wait until they pop. Add the ginger and chillies and fry them for a couple of seconds. Mix this into the mashed potato and add salt, lemon juice and fresh coriander. Form the mixture into small balls about 2.5 cm (1 in) in diameter.

For the batter, mix the flour, salt, oil and water until smooth. Dip the potato balls into the batter and deep-fry them until golden.

If the batter is runny, add more chickpea flour so that it sticks to the potato balls and does not splatter into the hot oil.

Serve hot with Tomato Sauce (page 89).

MAKES 20-25 BALLS.

BALLS
1 kg (2 lb) potatoes boiled and mashed
oil, for frying
½ tsp mustard seeds
1 tbs ginger, grated finely
2 fresh green chillies, seeded and chopped
1 level tsp salt, to taste
juice of ½ lemon
1 tbs fresh coriander, chopped

BATTER
180 g (6 oz) chickpea flour
1 level tsp salt
1 tbs of oil
150 ml (¼ pint) water
oil, for deep frying

Desserts

Apple Crunch

Peel and slice the apples and put them into a pan with 3-4 tablespoons sugar and the water. Cook until soft. Break the bread into pieces and grind into crumbs. Melt the butter or margarine in a saucepan, add the breadcrumbs and demerara sugar and cook gently over a low heat until golden brown. Leave to cool. Arrange layers of breadcrumb mixture and apples in a glass dish, finishing with a layer of breadcrumbs. Chill in the refrigerator. Whip the cream and spread on top of the crumbs. Sprinkle grated chocolate over the cream.

500 g (1 lb) cooking apples
2 tbs water
3-4 tbs sugar
125 g (4 oz) brown bread
60 g (2 oz) butter OR margarine
60 g (2 oz) demerara sugar
150 ml (¼ pint) whipping cream
60 g (2 oz) plain chocolate, grated

SERVES 4-6.

Baked Apples (Opposite)

Set the oven to 190°C/375°F/Gas Mark 5. Wash the apples and remove the cores using an apple corer. Place the apples on a baking tray. Combine sugar, raisins or sultanas and golden syrup and fill the centres with this mixture. Bake for 20- 30 minutes until cooked.

4 cooking apples
3 tbs brown sugar
90 g (3 oz) raisins OR sultanas
3 tbs golden syrup

Serve warm.

SERVES 4.

Baked Bananas

Slice each banana in half lengthwise and then again across the width. Place in an ovenproof dish and cover with butter or margarine, sugar and lemon juice. Bake in the oven at 200°C/400°F/Gas Mark 6 for 15 minutes, turning once or twice.

3 large bananas
60 g (2 oz) butter OR margarine
60 g (2 oz) sugar
2 tbs lemon juice
300 ml (½ pint) whipped cream

Serve with whipped cream.

SERVES 3.

Apple Pie

Prepare the pastry by sifting the flour and salt, and rubbing in the butter or margarine until the mixture resembles fine breadcrumbs. Add sufficient cold water to make a firm dough. Roll out thinly and evenly. Line a 25 cm (10 in) flan dish with pastry. Line the flan pastry with greaseproof paper or aluminium foil and fill with dried beans. Bake blind in a hot oven at 200°C/400°F/Gas Mark 6 for 10 minutes. Remove the beans and paper or foil. Keep the beans to use again.

Fill the pastry crust with apple pulp. Sprinkle cinnamon and sultanas.

Mix oats, butter or margarine and sugar together and spread over the top. Alternatively, make lattice strips from leftover pastry and sprinkle with sugar. Bake at 180°C/350°F/Gas Mark 4 for 30 minutes.

Serve with cream.

SERVES 8-10.

BASE

300 g (10 oz) flour, wholemeal or plain
pinch of salt
150 - 175 g (5 - 6 oz) butter OR margarine
cold water, to mix
dried beans, for baking blind

FILLING

420 g (14 oz) apples, cooked and pulped
1 tsp cinnamon, ground
2 tbs sultanas

TOPPING

125 g (4 oz) oats
150 g (5 oz) butter OR margarine
1 tbs muscovado sugar

Banana Pudding

Peel bananas and slice 1 cm (½ in) thick. Arrange in a 20 x 25 cm (8 x 10 in) baking dish. Mix coconut, sugar, cardamom and cashews together and spread over the sliced bananas. Pour the coconut milk over the top. Bake at 150°C/300°F/Gas Mark 2 until the moisture is absorbed and the bananas are cooked. Garnish with pistachios.

Serve with double cream.

SERVES 4-6.

4-6 large bananas
125 g (4 oz) desiccated coconut
60 g (2 oz) brown sugar
¼ tsp cardamom, ground
1 tbs cashew nuts, ground
500 ml (16 fl oz) coconut milk
1 tbs pistachio nuts, chopped
300 ml (½ pint) double cream

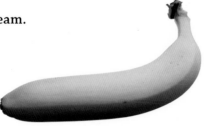

Christmas Pudding

Mix the flour, baking powder and breadcrumbs together. In a separate bowl, mix the remaining ingredients thoroughly. Stir in the flour and breadcrumb mixture. Transfer the pudding mixture to a greased heat proof bowl, leaving 5 cm (2 in) at the top to allow for rising. Cover with foil, secured with a rubber band, and steam for 6-8 hours. The pudding may be kept for a week or two. It should be steamed for an hour before using.

Serve with Custard or Date Sauce (see below).

SERVES 6-8.

60 g (2 oz) 100% wholemeal flour
½ tsp baking powder
125 g (4 oz) 100% wholemeal breadcrumbs
90 g (3 oz) sultanas
90 g (3 oz) currants
180 g (6 oz) seeded raisins
1 tsp orange peel, grated
2 tbs lemon juice
½ tsp mixed spice
125 ml (4 fl oz) soya milk
90 ml (3 fl oz) vegetable oil
1 tbs molasses

Custard

Mix the custard powder in a bowl with 2 tablespoons of cold milk. Heat up the remainder of the milk. When it is warm, remove from the heat. Add the sugar and stir. Add the custard powder and whisk vigorously to a smooth consistency. Return the custard to the heat and bring to the boil. Remove from the heat and add the nutmeg and/or vanilla essence.

MAKES 1 PINT OF CUSTARD.

600 ml (1 pint) cold milk
2 ½ tbs custard powder
2 tbs sugar
1 pinch of nutmeg and/or a few drops of vanilla essence

Date Sauce

Liquidise dates in soya milk and discard any coarse pieces. Mix the cornflour into a smooth paste with 4 tablespoons of soya milk. Heat the date mixture to boiling point, then add the cornflour paste, stirring vigorously. Sweeten to taste with brown sugar and flavour with vanilla.

SERVE ON CHRISTMAS PUDDING.

125 g (4 oz) dates
600 ml (1 pint) soya milk
125 g (4 oz) cornflour
4 tbs brown sugar
1 tsp vanilla essence

Fried Pineapple

Skin and cut the pineapple into small chunks. Place the butter or margarine and sugar in a frying pan over a low heat until the sugar has dissolved. Add pineapple chunks and cook for a further 15 minutes, stirring occasionally until the pineapple chunks are coated. Add orange juice and coconut, stir and leave to cool. Whip the double cream until it thickens.

Serve the coated pineapple chunks with cream.

SERVES 5-6.

500 g (1 lb) fresh pineapple
30-60 g (1-2 oz) butter OR margarine
90 g (3 oz) light brown sugar
3 tbs orange juice
2-3 tbs desiccated coconut
250 ml (8 fl oz) double cream

Fruit Cream Delight

Blend most of the strawberries, sugar, grape juice and half of the cream. Place half the jam in 6 small dessert bowls, cover with half the apricots and then half the blended mixture. Repeat the layers, finishing with cream. Refrigerate. Just before serving, decorate with 1 or 2 fresh strawberries.

SERVES 6.

450 g (15 oz) strawberries
2 tsp sugar
1 tbs black grape juice
250 ml (8 fl oz) whipped cream
150 g (5 oz) Strawberry Jam (page 210)
150 g (5 oz) fresh apricots, chopped

Fruit Cream Dessert

Chop the fruit into small cubes. Mix sour cream and yoghurt in a separate bowl and add vanilla, nutmeg and sugar according to taste. Add fruit and mix. Serve chilled.

SERVES 4.

500 g (1 lb) fresh fruit of your choice
150 ml (¼ pint) sour cream
150 ml (¼ pint) plain yoghurt
1 tsp vanilla essence
pinch of nutmeg, ground
125 g (4 oz) brown sugar

Fruit Crumble

Set the oven to 180°C/350°F/Gas Mark 4. Sprinkle the fruit with half the sugar. Mix and place in a 25 cm (10 in) baking dish. Prepare the crumble by mixing flour and remaining sugar in a mixing bowl, rubbing in butter or margarine until the mixture resembles breadcrumbs, and adding oats. Sprinkle the crumble mixture over the fruit. Bake for 20-30 minutes or until light golden brown. Sprinkle with demerara sugar.

Serve with fresh cream or Custard (page 119).

SERVES 4-6.

500 g (1 lb) fresh fruit, finely chopped
— citrus fruit is unsuitable
125 g (4 oz) sugar
125 g (4 oz) plain flour
1 tbs mixed spice (optional)
60 g (2 oz) butter OR margarine
60 g (2 oz) rolled oats
1 tbs demerara sugar

Fruit Juice Jelly

Blend the agar agar to a smooth paste with a little of the water. Add the remaining water and the fruit juice, transfer to a pan and bring to the boil. Remove from the heat and pour into a mould. When cool put in the refrigerator and leave to set.

SERVES 2-4.

3 tsp agar agar
300 ml (½ pint) water
300 ml (½ pint) fruit juice

Fruit Salad—Fresh

Halve the grapes and dice all the fruit. Soak the raisins in apple or orange juice for 1 hour. Mix all these ingredients together. Add sugar and sprinkle with coconut. Add more juice if necessary.

Serve with fresh cream, Yoghurt (page 212) or Custard (page 119).

SERVES 6-8.

125 g (4 oz) seedless grapes
2 bananas
4 peaches
2 ripe pears
125 g (4 oz) raisins
600 ml (1 pint) apple OR orange juice
sugar, to taste
1 tbs desiccated coconut

Fruit Salad—Grated

Grate pears and apples and sprinkle with lemon juice. Place in small dessert bowls and drizzle with honey. Sprinkle with nuts and cinnamon.

Quantities of honey, nuts and cinnamon can be varied according to taste. Use a combination of almonds, hazelnuts and walnuts.

SERVES 4-5.

2 conference pears
2 eating apples
juice of ½ lemon
2 tbs honey
60 g (2 oz) mixed nuts, coarsely chopped
1 tsp cinnamon, ground

Fruit Shortbread

Set the oven to 180°C/350°F/Gas Mark 4. Mix the flours and sugar and rub in the butter or margarine until the mixture resembles breadcrumbs. Press the mixture into a 28 cm (11 in) baking tray. Bake for 20 minutes until golden brown.

Cover with jam. Spread drained pineapple over the jam. Sprinkle sugar over the fruit and serve.

Serve with fresh cream.

Serves 5-6.

180 g (6 oz) flour
1 tbs rice flour
60 g (2 oz) icing sugar
125 g (4 oz) butter OR margarine

FILLING
250-315 g (8-10 oz) Apricot Jam
(page 210)
400 g (13 oz) canned pineapple,
small chunks
60 g (2 oz) sugar

Halva (Opposite)

Melt the butter or margarine in a fairly large saucepan over a low heat. Add in the semolina and stir continuously until golden brown. Reduce the heat and then gently pour in the hot water or milk, stirring all the time until the hot water or milk is absorbed in the semolina taking care not to burn it. Add sugar, almonds, cardamom and sultanas/raisins. Mix everything together, and cook the halva until it comes away from the sides of the pan.

Serve hot.

SERVES 6-7.

125g (8oz) butter
125g (8oz) coarse semolina
1litre (1.75 pints) hot water or milk
180g (6oz) sugar
30g (1oz) chopped almonds
½ level tsp ground cardamom
30g (2oz) sultanas/raisins

Ice Cream

Place the can of evaporated milk in a freezer for about an hour. Cream it with an electric mixer until light and fluffy. Add the double cream and vanilla essence and whisk until thick. Add the sugar and mix well. Pour it into a plastic container and decorate with nuts and glacé cherries. Place the container in the freezer to set.

Vanilla essence can be replaced by any flavour of your choice.

SERVES 6.

300 ml (½ pint) canned unsweetened
  evaporated milk
600 ml (1 pint) double cream
1½ tsp vanilla essence
10-12 tbs caster sugar
mixed nuts, chopped for decoration
  (optional)
glacé cherries for decoration (optional)

Ice Cream—Chocolate

Heat the milk, sugar and chocolate together without letting them boil and allow the milk to cool before adding to the cream. Whisk the cream until it is quite thick. Add milk, sugar and chocolate to the cream. Stir and put into a plastic container and freeze.

150 ml (¼ pint) milk
60 g (2 oz) caster sugar
300 ml (½ pint) double cream
60 g (2 oz) chocolate

Ice Cream—Chocolate with Almonds

Mix together single cream, double cream and condensed milk until aerated and only half way to thickening. Put the cocoa powder into a small bowl and slowly add enough boiling water to make a thick paste.

Add the mixture to the cream and milk. Stir well and add vanilla or almond essence and almonds. Place the mixture into a plastic container and freeze.

300 ml (½ pint) single cream
300 ml (½ pint) double cream
375 ml (12 oz) sweetened condensed milk
1½-2 tsp cocoa powder
boiling water, to mix
1 tsp vanilla or almond essence
roasted almonds, chopped (optional)

Jam Tart

Combine flour, salt and sugar. Rub in the oil or margarine and then mix in the water to create a soft dough. Roll it out to 1 cm (½ in) thick. Oil and flour a round baking tray. Line the tray with the pastry and trim off the excess pastry. Prick the dough with a fork. Spread the jam on top evenly with a knife. Decorate with pastry strips.

Bake at 190°C/375°F/Gas Mark 5 for approximately 20 minutes, until the pastry is cooked.

Serve with cream or Custard (page 119). SERVES 4-6.

250 g (8 oz) self-raising flour
pinch of salt
30 g (1 oz) sugar
125 g (4 oz) oil OR margarine
Cold water, to mix
jam, for the filling (page 206-210)

Lemon Flan

Melt the butter or margarine. Crush the biscuits into crumbs and mix with the butter or margarine. Press the mixture into a lightly greased 20 x 25 cm (8 x 10 in) flan case. Whip together cream, condensed milk and lemon juice. Spoon into the flan case and chill.

SERVES 4-6.

125 g (4 oz) butter OR margarine
250 g (8 oz) ginger biscuits (page 151)
150 ml (¼ pint) double cream
400 g (14 oz) sweetened condensed milk
1-2 tbs lemon juice to taste

Mince Pies

Sift the flour, add the sugar and rub the butter or margarine and fat into the flour. Add the water to form a dough. As the pastry is extra rich, it is important to allow it to become firm in the refrigerator for at least 30 minutes. Roll the pastry out onto a floured board and cut into 24 rounds. Put into greased cupcake trays, fill with mincemeat. Re-roll the remaining trimmings and cut out circles using a slightly smaller cutter. Dampen the edges of the circle with water and place on the pies and seal.

Bake at 400°F/200°C/Gas Mark 6 for 25 minutes. Allow to cool, then dredge the tops with icing sugar.

MAKES 24 MINCE PIES.

500 g (1 lb) plain flour
60 g (2 oz) caster sugar
250 g (½ lb) butter OR margarine
90 g (3 oz) vegetable fat
2 tbs water
Mincemeat (page 205)
icing sugar, to dust

Mince Tart

Sift the flour, rub in the fat and add water to bind into firm dough. Refrigerate for half an hour. Roll out on a floured board to cover a 20 or 23 cm (8 or 9 in) pie dish. Fill generously with Mincemeat. Top with strips of pastry over the mincemeat to make a lattice and bake at 200°C/400°F/Gas Mark 6 for about 30 minutes. Allow to cool on a wire rack.

Serve with Custard (page 119).

SERVES 4-6.

PASTRY
250 g (8 oz) self-raising flour
125 g (4 oz) vegetable fat
3-4 tbs cold water to bind
410 g (13 oz) Mincemeat (page 205)

Peach Sorbet

Make the syrup by combing water and sugar in a small saucepan and bring to boil stirring until the sugar has dissolved. Remove from the heat and leave to cool. Purée the peaches in a blender. Mix the syrup and peach purée together. Add lemon juice to taste. Pour into a freezing tray or plastic container and leave in the ice making compartment of a refrigerator until frozen.

SERVES 6-8.

150 ml (¼ pint) water
45 g (1½ oz) granulated sugar
500 g (1 lb) canned peaches
2-2½ tsp lemon juice

Stuffed Pears

Set the oven to 180°C/350°F/Gas Mark 4. Wash and core the pears using an apple corer. Mix the sugar, dates and nuts together. Place the cored pears on a greased baking tray and stuff with the nut and date mixture. Bake for 20-25 minutes.

Serve hot or cold.

SERVES 4.

4 firm pears
60 g (2 oz) sugar
90 g (3 oz) dates, chopped
60 g (2 oz) mixed nuts, chopped

Strawberry Tarts

Sift flour, sugar and salt into a mixing bowl. Cut the butter in small cubes and rub into the flour until the mixture looks like breadcrumbs. Gradually add water until a firm dough is formed. Keep the dough in the refrigerator for 30-45 minutes before rolling it out. Roll out the pastry to 5 mm (¼ in) thick. Cut out rounds with a pastry cutter and line the greased tart tin with pastry.

Bake at 200°C/400°F/Gas Mark 6 for 12 minutes or until light golden brown in a hot oven. Leave to cool. Whip the double cream with the vanilla essence. Fill each tart with one or two strawberries and a teaspoonful of whipped cream, then sprinkle with caster sugar.

MAKES 10 TARTS.

125 g (4 oz) plain flour
45 g (2 oz) sugar
½ tsp salt
60 g (2 oz) butter OR margarine
cold water, to mix
450 ml (¾ pint) double cream
¼ tsp vanilla essence
500 g (1 lb) fresh strawberries
caster sugar, for sprinkling

Sweet Vermicelli

Melt the butter or margarine in a saucepan, add the vermicelli and fry until golden brown. Pour in the milk and cook the vermicelli for 30 minutes or until cooked, stirring gently from time to time. Add the sugar, cardamom and nuts. Simmer until the milk thickens slightly.

SERVES 6-8.

60 g (2 oz) butter OR margarine
125 g (4 oz) vermicelli
900 ml (1½ pints) milk
180 g (6 oz) sugar
½ tsp cardamom, ground
60 g (2 oz) almonds, chopped
60 g (2 oz) pistachios, chopped

Tapioca Pudding

Wash the tapioca in cold water. Bring the milk to the boil, add the tapioca and stir continuously until it is cooked and the tapioca becomes translucent. Add sugar, cardamom and almonds to taste.

SERVES 4.

60 g (2 oz) tapioca (small or large grains)
600 ml (1 pint) milk
30-60 g (1-2 oz) almonds, chopped
sugar, to taste
½ tsp cardamom, ground

127

Trifle

Cover the base of a bowl with pieces of sponge cake. Mix all the fruits and spread evenly over the sponge cake. Prepare the jelly, pour it onto the fruit and leave it to set in the refrigerator for 1 hour. Meanwhile, prepare the custard and allow it to cool. Completely cover the jelly and cake with custard. Whip the double cream and spread it evenly over the custard. Sprinkle with grated chocolate and leave in the refrigerator for 1 hour before serving.

SERVES 8-10.

Plain Sponge Cake (page 134)
60 g (2 oz) seedless grapes, halved
185 g (6 oz) canned peaches
185 g (6 oz) canned pineapple
600 ml (1 pint) Fruit Juice Jelly
   (page 121)
600 ml (1 pint) Custard (page 119)
300 ml (½ pint) double cream
60 g (2 oz) cooking chocolate, grated

Yoghurt Ice

Keep a few strawberries for decoration. Place all the ingredients in a blender and liquidise, then pour into small serving bowls. Freeze for 3-4 hours in the freezer. Decorate with strawberries before serving.

SERVES 4-6.

500 g (1 lb) fresh strawberries
300 ml (½ pint) natural yoghurt
2 tbs golden syrup
250 ml (8 fl oz) double cream

Yoghurt Orange Whip

Peel the oranges and save the peel. Chop the flesh and blend with honey and yoghurt in the blender. Chill and top with nuts and grated orange rind.

SERVES 4.

8 oranges
2 tbs honey
600 ml (1 pint) yoghurt
nuts, chopped for topping

Cakes, Biscuits and Decorations

Apple Cake

Set the oven temperature to midway between 160°C/325°F/Gas Mark 3 and 180°C/350°F/Gas Mark 4. Grease two 25 cm (10 in) cake tins and line them with greaseproof paper.

Peel the apples and remove the cores. Chop roughly into slices and put into a pan with 2 tablespoons of water. Cover and stew until soft. Meanwhile, cream the fat and sugar together in a bowl large enough to hold the whole of the cake mixture. Sift the flour into a separate bowl with the mixed spice, baking powder. Add the walnuts and raisins or other dried fruit. By now, the apples should be cooked and cooled. Add the cooked apples to the bowl and mix thoroughly with a wooden spoon. Place the cake mixture in the cake tins and level the top. Decorate with almonds, if desired. Place the cake tins just above the centre of the oven, and bake for about 30-35 minutes, or until the knife inserted in the centre comes out clean. Leave to cool before turning out.

Non-stick tins should be greased lightly. Other tins should be lined with greaseproof paper or a silicon-treated baking parchment.

MAKES 2 CAKES.

1 kg (2 lb) cooking apples
2 tbs water
150 g (5 oz) soft white vegetable fat
375 g (12 oz) brown sugar
750 g (1½ lb) self-raising flour
2 tsp mixed spice
1 tsp baking powder
60 g (2 oz) walnuts, chopped
375 g (12 oz) raisins OR other dried fruit
almonds, flaked, for decoration (optional)

Simple Chocolate Cake (Opposite)

Set the oven to 180°C/350°F/Gas Mark 4. Melt the butter or margarine for 2 minutes in the microwave and pour into a large mixing bowl. Add condensed milk, vanilla essence and half the milk and beat together. Add the cocoa powder and the sponge flour or self-raising flour and baking powder slowly, using a spatula to fold in the mixture with the other half of the milk. The texture should be smooth and of dropping consistency. Cover a 20-25 cm (8-10 in) baking tin with greaseproof paper and spread the mixture evenly 2 cm (1 in) deep equally over the tin. Bake for 30-35 minutes or until the knife inserted in the centre comes out clean. When it comes out of the oven, place another tray over it, turn it over and peel off the greaseproof paper. When the cake has cooled, cover with cling film to keep it moist.

The top can be iced with Chocolate Icing (page 158). For a coffee and chocolate flavoured cake, add 2 teaspoons of diluted coffee.

150 g (5 oz) butter OR margarine
400 g (14 oz) sweetened condensed milk
1 tsp vanilla essence
250 ml (8 fl oz) milk
4 tbs cocoa powder
300 g (10 oz) sponge flour OR
300 g (10 oz) self-raising flour
½ tsp baking powder

Plain Sponge Cake

Sift the flour, custard powder, salt, baking powder and bicarbonate of soda into a bowl. Whisk the milk, oil, yoghurt, golden syrup and vanilla essence together in another bowl. Add the caster sugar and whisk further.

Add in the dry ingredients and mix well to form a smooth mixture. Pour this mixture into a greased 23 cm (9 in) cake tin and bake in a hot oven at 180°C/350°F/Gas Mark 4 for about 25-30 minutes, or until the knife inserted in the centre comes out clean.

Variation: add 3 tbs cocoa powder with the flour.

375 g (12 oz) sponge flour OR
*   self-raising flour*
2 tbs custard powder
½ tsp salt
2 level baking powder
1 tsp bicarbonate of soda
450 ml (¾ pint) milk
180 ml (6 fl oz) oil
2 tsp vanilla essence
2 tbs plain yoghurt
3 tbs golden syrup
180 g (6 oz) caster sugar

Chocolate Sponge Sandwich

Sift flour, cocoa, sugar, baking powder and bicarbonate of soda into a bowl. Put the butter or margarine, syrup, and milk and water into a small saucepan and cook over a very gentle heat until the butter or margarine has melted. When just tepid, add the dry ingredients and mix to a smooth batter with a wooden spoon.

Turn into a 20 x 5 cm (8 x 2 in) greased sandwich tin, and bake at 180°C/350°F/Gas Mark 4 for 20 minutes, or until the knife inserted in the centre comes out clean and dry. Cool on a rack and, when cold, cut in half and spread with Chocolate Icing. The top can also be iced or simply sprinkled with icing sugar.

FOR A STEAMED CHOCOLATE SPONGE SANDWICH
This is a useful alternative if an oven is not available. Turn the mixture into a greased cake tin 13 cm (5 in) in diameter and cover with greased paper. Place in a steamer, cover with a tightly fitting lid and steam gently over boiling water for 1 hour. Remove the paper cover and leave to stand for a few minutes before turning out. Cool on a wire rack.

150 g (5 oz) self-raising flour
30 g (1 oz) cocoa
30 g (1 oz) sugar
½ tsp bicarbonate of soda
1 level tsp baking powder
60 g (2 oz) butter OR
*   margarine*
1 tbs golden syrup
6 tbs milk and water, mixed
Chocolate Icing (page 158) OR
*   icing sugar, for sprinkling*

Chocolate Sponge Sandwich with Fruit

Heat the milk in a saucepan until warm, add bicarbonate of soda and set aside for 15 minutes. Sift flour and sugar into a bowl. Mix margarine and condensed milk together and add in the warm milk. Add in the flour and sugar and blend with a hand blender, until the mixture is of dropping consistency.

Bake at 160°C/320°F/Gas Mark 4 for 25-30 minutes, or until the knife inserted in the centre comes out clean.

Chocolate Sponge Sandwich. While the cakes are in the oven, prepare the filling. Whip the cream until stiff. Sift the icing sugar into the cream, and add the fruit. Mix well. Allow the cakes to cool in their tins until completely cold, then turn out one cake onto a plate or cake board. Spread the whipped cream filling over it. Place the second cake on top. Dust with icing sugar.

MAKES 2 LARGE SANDWICHES.

1kg (2lb) supreme sponge flour or
*   self-raising flour*
60 g (2 oz) cocoa
250 g (½ lb) sugar
4 level tsp bicarbonate of soda
500 g (1lb) margarine
2 cans of condensed milk
2 tsp Vanilla essence
900 ml 1½ pint warm milk
Chocolate Icing (page 158) OR
*   icing sugar, for sprinkling*

FILLING
150 ml (¼ pint) double or whipping cream
1 tbs icing sugar
125 g (4 oz) strawberries OR 125 g (4 oz)
*   raspberries*
*   OR 1 peeled mango, finely cubed*
icing sugar, for decoration

Christmas Cake

Mix the molasses, lemon juice, orange rind, oil, soya milk and fruits together thoroughly. Sift the flour, baking powder and mixed spice together and stir into the fruit mixture. Turn into a 20 cm (8 in) non-stick cake tin.

Bake at 150°C/300°F/Gas Mark 2 for 3 hours. Cover with greaseproof paper, and bake at 120°C/250°F/Gas Mark ½ for another hour or until a skewer inserted into the cake comes out clean and dry. Decorate with nuts, if desired, or cover with marzipan.

1 tbs molasses
1 tbs lemon juice
1 tsp orange rind, grated
125 ml (4 fl oz) vegetable oil
300 ml (½ pint) soya milk
250 g (8 oz) currants
250 g (8 oz) sultanas
125 g (4 oz) seeded raisins
375 g (12 oz) wholemeal flour
2 tsp baking powder
1 tsp mixed spice
chopped nuts and marzipan for decoration
*   (optional)*

Carrot Cake

Set the oven to 190°C/375°F/Gas Mark 5. Mix the sugar, oil, vinegar, milk and vanilla in a large bowl. Sift flours, salt, bicarbonate of soda, cinnamon and baking powder into the mixture. Add the carrots, pecans or walnuts and pineapple and mix well. Transfer to a greased 20 cm (8 in) cake tin. Bake in the oven for 25-30 minutes, or until the knife inserted in the centre comes out clean and dry. Allow to cool before removing from the tin.

Beat the butter, cream cheese, vanilla, icing sugar together and add nuts. Mix and spread evenly over the cooled cake.

Any variety of nuts can be used for decoration.

125 g (4 oz) sugar
125 ml (4 fl oz) vegetable oil
4 tsp malt vinegar
180 ml (6 fl oz) milk
1 tsp vanilla essence
125 g (4 oz) white self-raising flour
125 g (4 oz) wholemeal self-raising flour
1 tsp salt
2 tsp cinnamon
2 tsp cinnamon
1 tsp baking powder
375 g (12 oz) carrot, grated
125 g (4 oz) pecan OR walnuts, chopped
125 g (4 oz) pineapple, crushed (no juice)

FROSTING
125 g (4 oz) butter
250 g (8 oz) cream cheese
1 tsp vanilla essence
250 g (8 oz) icing sugar
125 g (4 oz) nuts, chopped

Chocolate Sponge Cake

Put the chocolate, butter or margarine and milk into a saucepan and melt over a low heat (it should not boil). Mix well and leave to cool a little. Sift the flour, salt, baking powder and bicarbonate of soda together in a bowl. Stir in the sugar. Add the vanilla to the chocolate and gradually mix the melted ingredients into the dry ingredients. Spoon into a greased and paper lined, round 20 cm (8 in) cake tin.

Bake at 170°C/340°F/Gas Mark 4 for 25-30 minutes or until the knife inserted in the centre comes out clean and dry. Leave to cool before turning out.

60 g (2 oz) plain chocolate
90 g (3 oz) butter OR margarine
250 ml (8 fl oz) milk
210 g (7 oz) self-raising flour
pinch of salt
1 tsp baking powder
125 g (4 oz) sugar
1 tsp vanilla essence

Date Cake

Put the dates, bicarbonate of soda and water into a small saucepan, bring slowly to the boil, simmer very gently for 5 minutes and then leave to cool. Sift the flour and mixed spice, add sugar into a bowl and rub in the butter or margarine. Pour the date mixture into the flour and mix thoroughly with a wooden spoon. Turn into a greased shallow tin 20 x 5 cm (8 x 2 in), spread smoothly with a wet knife and bake at 190°C/375°F/ Gas Mark 5 for 30 minutes, or until the knife inserted in the centre comes out clean and dry. Leave to cool before turning out.

125 g (4 oz) dates, chopped
60 ml (2 fl oz) water
150 g (5 oz) self-raising flour
¼ tsp mixed spice
60 g (2 oz) sugar
1 tsp bicarbonate of soda
60 g (2 oz) butter OR margarine

Fruit Cake

Rub the butter or margarine into the flour. Add the sugar, currants, sultanas, candied peel and milk and mix thoroughly. Dissolve the bicarbonate of soda in water and add to the mixture. Then add the vinegar. Turn into a 18 cm (7 in) diameter cake tin lined with greaseproof paper and bake at 150°C/300°F/Gas Mark 5 for 1 hour, or until the knife inserted in the centre comes out clean and dry. Leave to cool before turning out.

125 g (4 oz) butter OR margarine
250 g (8 oz) plain flour
90 g (3 oz) soft brown sugar
90 g (3 oz) currants
125 g (4 oz) sultanas
30 g (1 oz) candied peel
150 ml (¼ pint) milk
1 tbs bicarbonate of soda
1 tbs tepid water
1 tbs malt or balsamic vinegar

Walnut Cake

Melt the butter or margarine and beat in the sugar and evaporated milk. Add the flour, baking powder, salt and vanilla essence and gradually mix in the nuts and the milk. Transfer to a greased 25 cm (10 in) baking tin and bake at 180°C/350°F/ Gas Mark 4 for 35-40 minutes, or until the knife inserted in the centre comes out clean and dry. Leave to cool before removing from the tin.

90 g (3oz) chopped walnuts
125 g (4 oz) butter OR margarine
270 g (9 oz) sugar
125 ml (4 fl oz) evaporated milk
570 g (19 oz) self-raising flour
1 tsp baking powder
pinch of salt
1 tsp vanilla essence
180 ml (6 fl oz) milk

Cheesecake (Opposite)

Mix the flour, mixed nuts, butter and sugar together and press into a greased and lined 20 cm (8 in) tin. Bake at 180°C/350°F/Gas Mark 4 for 20 minutes. Allow to cool.

Mix together cream cheese, lemon peel, grated lemon juice, sugar, vanilla essence, yoghurt and milk. Pour on top of the base and bake at 160°C/325°F/Gas Mark 3 for 25 minutes. Cool for 5 minutes.

Mix together sour cream, sugar and vanilla, pour over the cheesecake and bake at 160°C/325°F/Gas Mark 3 for 7 minutes. Leave to cool in the refrigerator for a minimum of 2 hours before serving.

The Cheesecake can be decorated with pistachios, fruit or fruit jam.

BASE

180 g (6 oz) plain flour
60 g (2 oz) mixed nuts, (walnuts, cashews and almonds) finely chopped
90 g (3 oz) butter, melted

FILLING

500 g (1 lb) cream cheese
2 tsp lemon peel, grated
1½ tbs lemon juice
90 g (3 oz) sugar
1½ tsp vanilla essence
2 tbs plain yoghurt
5 tbs milk

TOPPING

500 ml (16 oz) sour cream
45 g (1½ oz) sugar
2 tsp vanilla essence

Fruit Loaf

Mix the bran, sugar and fruit well together in a bowl. Stir in the milk and leave to stand for half an hour. Sift in the flour, mixing well, and pour into a well greased 1 kg (2 lb) loaf tin.

Bake at 160°C/325°F/Gas Mark 4 for 35 minutes, or until a knife inserted into the cake comes out clean and dry. Leave to cool before turning out of the tin. Cut into slices.

125 g (4 oz) bran
150 g (5 oz) caster sugar
300 g (10 oz) mixed dried fruit
300 ml (½ pint) milk
125 g (4 oz) self-raising flour

Chocolate Burfi (Opposite)

Melt the butter in a saucepan, add the milk powder and coconut and cook over a low heat for 5 minutes. Add the milk, sugar, almonds and cardamom, stirring continuously until mixture becomes moist. Grease a baking sheet and a rolling pin with butter. Put the mixture onto the baking sheet and spread it evenly with the rolling pin. Allow the burfi to cool. Melt the chocolate over hot water and spread it evenly over the burfi. Allow the chocolate to set before cutting in small squares. Keep in the refrigerator.

60 g (2 oz) butter
250 ml (8 fl oz) milk
155 g (5 oz) coconut
250 g (8 oz) milk powder
185 g (6 oz) sugar
90 g (3 oz) almonds, ground
pinch of cardamom seeds, ground
250 g (8 oz) cooking chocolate
butter, for greasing

Sugarless Cake

Heat the dates and water gently in a saucepan until soft, then mash the dates into rough pieces. Mix the dried fruit, flour, baking powder, mixed spice, grated rind and orange juice in a bowl. Add dates water. Mix well and pour into a 1 kg (2 lb) loaf tin lined with greaseproof paper. Level the top and sprinkle with almonds.

Bake at 160°C/325°F/Gas Mark 3 for 1 hour, or until a skewer inserted into the cake comes out clean and dry. If the top of the cake is becoming too brown before the end of cooking time, cover it with greaseproof paper. Cool a little before turning out of the tin.

250 g (8 oz) cooking dates, chopped
300 ml (½ pint) water
500 g (1 lb) mixed dried fruit
180 g (6 oz) plain whole wheat flour
3 tsp baking powder
1 tsp mixed spice
rind of 1 orange OR lemon, grated
4 tbs orange juice
almonds, halved or chopped

Little Sesame Cakes

Set the oven at 180°C/350°F/Gas Mark 4. Heat the milk, water, oil and sugar gently in a saucepan until the sugar dissolves. Set aside to cool. Sift the flour with bicarbonate of soda, cinnamon and mixed spice or nutmeg into a bowl. Add the sesame seeds and currants. Add the liquid to the flour mixture and stir well. Add more water if necessary to make drop consistency. Put about 1 tablespoon of the mixture into each cake case. Bake for about 12-15 minutes or until a knifre inserted into the cake comes out clean and dry.

MAKES 48 SESAME CAKES.

300 ml (½ pint) milk
500 ml (16 fl oz) water
300 ml (½ pint) oil
500 g (1 lb) brown sugar
750 g (1½ lb) wholemeal flour
2 tsp bicarbonate of soda
2 tsp cinnamon, ground
1 tsp mixed spice OR nutmeg, ground
185 g (6 oz) sesame seeds
375 g (12 oz) currants

140

Quick Cherry Loaf (Opposite)

Set the oven to 180°C/350°F/Gas Mark 4. Prepare a 500 g (1lb) loaf tin by lightly greasing it and lining the base with greaseproof paper. Place all the ingredients, except the decoration and honey, in a bowl and mix well. Pour the mixture into the tin. Smooth out the top. Decorate with cherries and walnuts. Bake for 35-40 minutes, or until the knife inserted in the centre comes out clean and dry. Allow to cool. Brush with honey and cut into slices. To serve spread with butter or margarine.

250 ml (8 fl oz) milk
125 g (4 oz) glacé cherries, halved
125 g (4 oz) soft brown sugar
250 g (8 oz) self-raising flour
1 tsp mixed spice
½ tsp bicarbonate of soda
cherries and walnuts, halved for decoration
honey, to glaze

Orange and Coconut Cake

Make corn flour into a paste with a little water. Place the flour, baking powder, half of the coconut, butter or margarine, sugar, half of the orange rind, yoghurt in a bowl. Add the corn flour paste and mix well for 2-3 minutes, until a thick batter is formed. Grease two 18 cm (7 in) sandwich tins and line the base with greaseproof paper. Put the mixture into the tins and bake at 180°C/350°F/Gas Mark 4 for 30-35 minutes, or until the knife inserted in the centre comes out clean and dry. Allow it to cool.

Mix the icing sugar and orange juice or water together. Sandwich the 2 cakes together with a thin layer of the icing and spread the rest on top. Sprinkle with the remaining coconut and orange rind.

250 g (8 oz) self-raising flour
1 tsp baking powder
60 g (2 oz) desiccated coconut
250 g (8 oz) softened butter OR margarine
250 g (8 oz) sugar
rind of 2 oranges, grated
4 tbs plain yoghurt
4 tbs milk
4 tbs cornflour
125 g (4 oz) icing sugar
1-2 tbs orange juice OR water

Easy Cake (Opposite)

Mix the oil, orange juice and vanilla essence together in a mixing bowl. Stir in the flour and sugar. Mix well and pour into a greased, shallow 20 cm (8 in) cake tin and bake at 180°C/350°F/Gas Mark 6 for 30-35 minutes, or until a knife inserted into the cake comes out clean and dry. Leave to cool before removing from the tin.

250 ml (8 fl oz) cooking oil
250 ml (8 fl oz) fresh orange juice
½ tsp vanilla essence
400 g (13 oz) sponge flour OR
self-raising flour
125 g (4 oz) caster sugar

Tea Cakes

Mix the butter or margarine, sugar, nutmeg, colouring, custard powder, baking powder and vanilla together to a smooth, fluffy mixture. Add milk and mix. Gradually add flour, sultanas and coconut. Mix thoroughly and put tablespoons of the mixture into paper baking cases.

Bake at 190°C/375°F/Gas Mark 5 for 12-15 minutes, or until a knife inserted into the cake comes out clean and dry. Decorate cakes with own choice of decorations.

MAKES 50 TEA CAKES.

500 g (1 lb) butter OR margarine
625 g (1¼ lb) caster sugar
pinch of nutmeg, ground
1 tsp yellow food colouring
1½ tsp custard powder
1½ tsp baking powder
½ tsp vanilla essence
600 ml (1 pint) milk
1.125 kg (2¼ lb) self-raising flour
125 g (4 oz) sultanas
125 g (4 oz) coconut
almonds OR walnuts, chopped for
    decoration

Almond Biscuits

Mix the butter or margarine, sugar, vanilla essence or nutmeg, milk and bicarbonate of soda until creamy. Add the almonds and flour and roll into small balls.

Bake on a greased baking tray at 180°C/350°F/Gas Mark 4 for 15-20 minutes.

MAKES 50 BISCUITS.

500 g (1 lb) butter OR margarine
300 g (10 oz) sugar
1 tsp vanilla essence OR pinch of
*   nutmeg, ground*
125 ml (4 fl oz) milk
1 tsp bicarbonate of soda
500 g (1 lb) almonds, ground
1 kg (2 lb) plain flour, sifted

Banana Flapjacks

Grease an 18 x 28 cm (7 x 11 in) Swiss roll tin. Set the oven to 180°C/350°F/Gas Mark 4. Cream the butter or margarine until soft, then beat in the sugar, honey and banana. Stir in the flour and oats. Spoon into the Swiss roll tin and spread evenly. Bake towards the top of the oven for 25-30 minutes. Cut into fingers in the tin while still warm. Then leave to become quite cold before removing from the tin and separating the flapjacks.

MAKES 16-18 FLAPJACKS.

90 g (3 oz) butter OR margarine
125 g (4 oz) demerara sugar
1 tbs honey
1 banana, peeled and mashed
60 g (2 oz) plain flour
250 g (8 oz) rolled oats

Chocolate Coated Biscuits

Beat the butter or margarine, almond essence and sugar until creamy. Sift in the flour and form into a smooth paste. Spoon the mixture into a piping bag fitted with a large star nozzle. Pipe rounds onto 2 greased baking trays.

Bake at 160°C/325°F/Gas Mark 3 for 10-12 minutes or until lightly browned. Cool on baking trays until firm, then transfer to a wire rack and leave to cool.

Break the chocolate into a bowl and leave to melt over a pan of simmering water. Dip half of each biscuit into the chocolate. Leave the biscuits in a cool place until the chocolate has set.

MAKES 12 BISCUITS.

250 g (8 oz) softened butter OR
*   margarine*
¼ tsp almond essence
125 g (4 oz) caster sugar
250 g (8 oz) plain flour, sifted
125 g (4 oz) chocolate

Chocolate Chip Cookies

Beat the butter or margarine and sugar until creamy. Add all other ingredients, except milk, and mix well. Add sufficient milk to bind the mixture. Form into balls and place well apart on a greased tray.

Bake at 180°C/350°F/Gas Mark 4 for 10 minutes or until lightly browned.

MAKES 34-36 COOKIES.

125 g (4 oz) butter OR margarine
250 g (8 oz) brown sugar
1 tsp baking powder
75 g (2½ oz) coconut, shredded
75 g (2½ oz) rolled oats
60 g (2 oz) self-raising flour
125 g (4 oz) milk or white chocolate chips
2 tsp vanilla essence
125 g (4 oz) plain flour
milk, to mix

Chocolate Cookies

Mix the flour, almonds and salt together in a bowl. Rub in the butter or margarine. Divide into 2 parts. Add chocolate to 1 part. Work each part into a soft dough with milk and vanilla. Chill both both halves for 1 hour and knead each one separately, on a floured board. Roll out separately to a rectangle 5 mm (¼ in) thick. Place one on top of the other and roll them over together into a log shape. Chill for 30 minutes to make it easier to cut. With a sharp knife, cut into 1 cm (½ in) thick slices. Place flat on a greased baking tray.

Bake at 190°C/375°F/Gas Mark 5 for 20-25 minutes or until firm.

MAKES 15 COOKIES.

300 g (10 oz) plain flour, sifted
60 g (2 oz) almonds, ground
pinch of salt
180 g (6 oz) butter OR margarine
90 g (3 oz) plain chocolate, melted
milk, to mix
1 tsp vanilla essence

Chocolate Date Bars

Put the water, flour, dates, chocolate and vanilla in a small saucepan and cook for 10 minutes on low heat. Leave to cool.

To make the crumble, mix together the flour, oats and sugar in a bowl and rub in the butter or margarine. Spread half the crumble mixture over the base of a 25 x 30 cm (10 x 12 in) baking tin, pressing it down firmly. Cover with filling, then the remainder of the crumble. Press down with a rounded knife.

Bake at 190°C/375°F/Gas Mark 5 in the centre of the oven for about 25 minutes or until golden brown. Allow it to cool for 10 minutes, then turn out onto a board or other flat surface. Cut into fingers.

MAKES 12 FINGERS.

FILLING
150 ml (¼ pint) water
2 tsp flour
180 g (6 oz) pitted dates
125 g (4 oz) chocolate cooking
¼ tsp vanilla essence

CRUMBLE
125 g (4 oz) self-raising flour
150 g (5 oz) rolled oats
125 g (4 oz) light soft brown sugar
180 g (6 oz) butter OR margarine

Cocoa Biscuits

Place the butter or margarine, sugar, bicarbonate of soda, milk and vanilla or nutmeg in a bowl and mix. Add the flour and form into a soft dough. Divide the dough into 2 equal parts. Add cocoa powder to 1 part, kneading it until the cocoa powder is merged into the dough. Roll out each half separately, less than 5 mm (¼ in) thick. Place one on top of the other and roll them over together into a log shape. Cut the roll into slices, 1 cm (½ in) thick and place on a greased baking tray.

Bake at 180°C/350°F/Gas Mark 4 for 20-30 minutes.

MAKES 25-30 BISCUITS.

625 g (1 ¼ lb) butter OR margarine
500 g (1 lb) sugar
1 tsp bicarbonate of soda
1-2 tbs milk
1 tsp vanilla essence OR nutmeg, ground
1.25 kg (2½ lb) plain flour
3 tbs cocoa powder

Custard Powder Biscuits

Sift all the dry ingredients together. Rub in the butter or margarine. Knead very well without adding any liquid. Form into small balls. Place on a greased baking tray. Press down each ball with the back of a fork, crosswise.

Bake at 200°C/400°F/Gas Mark 6 for about 12 minutes.

MAKES 18-20 BISCUITS.

180 g (6 oz) plain flour
60 g (2 oz) custard powder
60 g (2 oz) icing sugar, sifted
1 tsp baking powder
pinch of salt
150 g (5 oz) butter OR margarine

Flapjacks

Melt the sugar, butter or margarine and syrup. Add oats and salt, mixing all the time. Press the mixture into a flat greased 25 x 28 (10 x 11 in) baking tray and bake at 180°C/350°F/Gas Mark 4 for 20 minutes. Allow to cool in the tray and cut into squares.

MAKES 12-16 FLAPJACKS.

250 g (8 oz) soft brown sugar
250 g (8 oz) butter OR margarine
4 tsp golden syrup
500 g (1 lb) rolled oats
pinch of salt

Finger Biscuits

Set the oven to 180°C/350°F/Gas Mark 4. Put the butter or margarine, sugar and syrup into a pan and heat gently until the butter has melted. Stir in the cinnamon, almonds, raisins, sesame seeds and oats and mix well. Roll out the pastry to 5 mm (¼ in) thick and line the bottom of a 25 x 28 cm (10 x 11 in) baking tray with it. Press the oats mixture down on top of the pastry using the back of a spoon.

To decorate, evenly space the glacé cherries on the top and bake in a hot oven at 180°C/350°F/Gas Mark 4 for 25-30 minutes. Whilst still warm, cut into slices. Allow to cool completely before removing from the tray.

MAKES 8-10 FINGER BISCUITS.

125 g (4 oz) butter OR margarine
125 g (4 oz) soft brown sugar
3 tbs golden syrup
1 tsp cinnamon, ground
60 g (2 oz) almonds, flaked
60 g (2 oz) raisins
60 g (2 oz) sesame seeds
90 g (3 oz) rolled oats
125 g (4 oz) puff pastry
6 glacé cherries, halved

Coconut Biscuits (Opposite)

Mix the butter or margarine, sugar, baking powder, custard powder and essence in a bowl. Add milk and mix until smooth. Add flour, coconut and semolina and form into a soft dough. Roll into small balls and place separately on a greased baking tray.

Bake at 180°C/350°F/Gas Mark 4 for 20-25 minutes.

MAKES 25-30 BISCUITS.

250 g (8 oz) butter OR margarine
60 g (2 oz) sugar
2 level tsp baking powder
3 tsp custard powder
½ tsp rose essence
125 ml (4 fl oz) milk
60 g (2 oz) plain flour
500 g (16 oz) desiccated coconut
60 g (2 oz) semolina

Ginger Biscuits

Set the oven to 190°C/375°F/Gas Mark 5. Mix the butter or margarine, sugar, golden syrup, ginger powder, baking powder, bicarbonate of soda and warm milk until soft and smooth. Add the flour and semolina and form a soft dough, adding more milk if needed. Roll out to 5 mm (¼ in) thick and cut with a biscuit cutter. Prick each biscuit with a fork and place on a greased baking tray. Bake for 15 minutes.

MAKES 25-30 BISCUITS.

250 g (8 oz) butter OR margarine
125 g (4 oz) brown sugar
4 tbs golden syrup
1½ tbs ginger powder
1½ tsp baking powder
1 tsp bicarbonate of soda
2 tbs warm milk
500 g (1 lb) plain flour
1 tbs semolina

Nutty Date Sweet (Opposite)

Melt the butter or margarine in a saucepan, add dates and cook over low heat until they begin to soften. Add nutmeg or cardamom and nuts. Mix thoroughly until all nuts are blended into the date mixture. Put the mixture on an oiled surface, oil the palms of your hands and roll out into two thick tubes and finally roll them in desiccated coconut. Place the rolls on a greased tray and refrigerate for 24 hours. Remove from the fridge, slice into 6 mm (¼ inch) thick rounds on the chopping board. Store in a tin.

Use the date blocks from the supermarkets for good results.

MAKES 25-30 PIECES.

60 g (2 oz) butter OR margarine
500 g (1 lb) dates block, chopped
pinch of nutmeg OR cardamom,
  ground
90 g (3 oz) almonds, chopped
90 g (3 oz) pistachios, chopped
90 g (3 oz) cashews, chopped
3 tbsp desiccated coconut

Hazelnut Squares

Cream the butter or margarine and the sugar. Stir in the flours and ground hazelnuts. Mix lightly. Add water to make into soft dough. Spread the dough evenly into a 25 x 30 cm (10 x 12 in) tin. Mark into squares and place a whole hazelnut on each square.

Bake at 150°C/300°F/Gas Mark 2 for 30-40 minutes until golden brown.

MAKES 16-18 SQUARES.

250 g (8 oz) butter OR margarine
60 g (2 oz) caster sugar
180 g (6 oz) plain flour
45 g (1½ oz) rice flour
125 g (4 oz) hazelnuts, ground
16-18 whole hazelnuts, roasted
water to mix

Oat Biscuits

Mix butter or margarine, sugar, bicarbonate of soda and honey or golden syrup until the mixture becomes fluffy. Add flour, coconut and oats, adding enough water to form into a soft dough. Take small amounts of the dough, shape them into rounds, slightly flatten and place on a greased baking tray and prick them with a fork.

Bake at 180°C/350°F/Gas Mark 4 for 15-20 minutes.

MAKES 30-35 BISCUITS.

500 g (1 lb) butter OR margarine
250 g (8 oz) sugar
1 tsp bicarbonate of soda
2 tbs honey OR golden syrup
625 g (1¼ lb) plain flour
250 g (8 oz) desiccated coconut
250 g (8 oz) rolled oats
water to mix

Oat Cakes

Mix oats, salt and baking powder. Rub in the butter or margarine. Add water to form a soft (but not sticky) dough. Roll out the dough to about 5mm thick, cut with a biscuit cutter and place on a greased baking tray. Prick with a fork.

Bake at 200°C/400°F/Gas Mark 6 for 15-20 minutes.

MAKES 25 OAT CAKES.

750 g (1½ lb) 'rolled' oats
1 tsp salt
2 tsp baking powder
155 g (5 oz) butter OR margarine
150 ml (5fl oz) water, to mix

Oatmeal Cookies

Mix the apple juice, salt and oil in a bowl. Stir in the oats and walnuts. Add enough flour to make a stiff dough. Form the dough into small balls and flatten each cookie with a fork. Place on a greased baking tray.

Bake at 190°C/375°F/Gas Mark 5 until golden brown.

MAKES 25 COOKIES.

75 ml (2½ fl oz) apple juice
½ tsp salt
4 tbs oil
500 g (1 lb) rolled oats
60 g (2 oz) walnuts, chopped
flour, to mix

Orange Shortcake Biscuits

Melt the butter or margarine. Mix all the dry ingredients in a large mixing bowl with the melted butter or margarine. Add the orange rind and the orange juice and mix. Roll out the mixture to a thickness of 8 cm (3 in) and place in the refrigerator for 2 hours. Cut it into 5 mm (¼ in) square slices and place apart on a greased baking tray.

Bake at 180°C/350°F/Gas Mark 4 for 15-20 minutes.

MAKES 8-10 BISCUITS.

210 g (7 oz) butter OR margarine
400 g (13 oz) plain flour
210 g (7 oz) sugar
1 tsp baking powder
½ tsp bicarbonate of soda
1 tsp orange rind, grated
60 ml (2 fl oz) orange juice

Pecan Puffs

Cream the sugar and butter or margarine together. Add vanilla essence and nuts. Slowly sift in the flour. Mix well. Roll into 2 cm (¾ in) balls and place them on a greased baking tray at 160°C/325°F/Gas Mark 3 for 30 minutes. When they are cool dust them with icing sugar.

MAKES 30 PUFFS.

60 g (2 oz) sugar
250 g (8 oz) butter OR margarine
2 tsp vanilla essence
150 g (5 oz) pecan nuts, ground
270 g (9 oz) wholemeal flour
icing sugar, for rolling
water to mix

Quick Peanut Butter Cookies

Combine all the ingredients in a large bowl and mix well. Place a tablespoon of mixture onto a greased baking tray to make 16-18 cookies. Flatten slightly with a fork and bake at 180°C/350°F/Gas Mark 4 for 10-12 minutes or until golden brown.

MAKES 16-18 COOKIES.

125 g (4 oz) peanut butter
60 g (2 oz) raisins
125 g (4 oz) self-raising flour
400 g (13 oz) sweetened condensed milk
1 tsp lemon juice
60 ml (2 fl oz) milk

Sesame Snaps

Melt the butter or margarine slowly over a low heat. Add the sugar and honey, stirring all the time with a wooden spoon. Add the sesame seeds and keep stirring to blend evenly. Add coconut and porridge oats stirring continuously. Press the mixture into a greased Swiss roll tin 33 x 23 cm (13 x 9 in).

Bake at 150°C/300°F/Gas Mark 2 for 30 minutes. Cut into squares when cool.

MAKES 24 SNAPS.

180 g (6 oz) butter OR margarine
90 g (3 oz) sugar
90 ml (3 fl oz) honey
60 g (2 oz) sesame seeds
140 g (4½ oz) desiccated coconut
180 g (6 oz) porridge oats

Shortbread

Set the oven to 160°C/325°F/Gas Mark 3. Sift the flours together and add the butter or margarine and sugar. Rub together with fingertips until the mixture begins to bind. Press the mixture into a 25 x 28 (10 x 11 in) greased baking tray. Prick the top of the mixture with a fork and bake for 30 minutes or until golden brown. Remove from the oven and allow to cool before cutting. Sprinkle caster sugar on top of the shortbread.

MAKES 16-20 SLICES.

250 g (8 oz) plain flour
125 g (4 oz) rice flour
250 g (8 oz) butter OR margarine
125 g (4 oz) sugar
caster sugar, for sprinkling

Star Biscuits (Opposite)

Set the oven to 180°C/350°F/Gas Mark 4. Sift the icing sugar into a bowl, add butter cut into pieces or margarine and cream together until light and fluffy. Sift in the flours and add water to make a smooth dough. Leave in the refrigerator to harden for 1 hour.

Place on a floured surface. Place the dough on a floured surface and roll out to 5mm thickness. Cut into star shapes using a star cutter. Place the stars on a greased baking tray and bake for 15-20 minutes.

Decorate with coloured icing and hundreds-and-thousands.

MAKES 24 BISCUITS.

250 g (8 oz) butter OR margarine
90 g (3 oz) icing sugar
250 g (8 oz) plain flour
125 g (4 oz) cornflour
2-4 tbs water

Butter Cream

Cream the butter until soft and gradually beat in the sugar, adding the milk and a few drops of vanilla essence.

125 g (4 oz) butter
180 g (6 oz) icing sugar
1-2 tbs milk
a few drops of vanilla essence

Chocolate Curls and Leaves (Opposite)

Chocolate curls are made by running a vegetable peeler or knife along the base of a bar of chocolate. Chocolate leaves are made by painting one side of clean, deep veined rose leaves with melted chocolate. Cool on waxed paper. Turn the chocolate leaves over, so that the chocolate side is on the palm of your hand and peel the leaf away carefully.

Chocolate

Chocolate Icing

Cream the butter until soft and gradually beat in the sugar, adding the milk and cocoa or drinking chocolate powder.

125 g (4 oz) butter
180 g (6 oz) icing sugar
1-2 tbs milk
2 tbs cocoa OR drinking chocolate
  powder

Grated Chocolate

Grate large pieces of chocolate, finely or coarsely, in a rotary hand grater, food processor or hand-grater. Rinse hands in cold water to prevent stickiness.

Chocolate

Treats

Almond Crunch

Dissolve the sugar in a pan over a low heat, add water and bring to the boil. Lower heat and add saffron, almonds and butter or margarine, stirring all the time. When the mixture thickens, pour into a greased dish, spread evenly and sprinkle the top with cardamom. Cut into squares.

MAKES 6-8 PIECES.

125 g (4 oz) sugar
5 tbs water
pinch of saffron
125 g (4 oz) almonds, chopped
125 g (4 oz) unsalted butter OR margarine
pinch of cardamom, ground

Banana Crunch

Put banana in a small bowl, cover with yoghurt and sprinkle with sugar, sultanas and wheat flakes.

SERVES 2.

1 banana, sliced
300 ml (½ pint) plain yoghurt
1 tbs sugar
30-60 g (1-2 oz) sultanas
30 g (1 oz) wheat flakes

Chocolate Rice Crisps (Opposite)

Break the chocolate into a large bowl and melt by placing over boiling water or putting in the microwave for 2 minutes. Mix in the Rice Crispies until thoroughly coated with chocolate. Whilst still warm, spoon the mixture into paper baking cases. Leave to cool.

Alternative: use cornflakes instead of Rice Crispies, but the cornflakes should be slightly crushed.

Decorate with hundreds and thousands, silver balls or decoration of your choice.

MAKES 50 CRISPS.

500 g (1 lb) cooking chocolate
330 g (11 oz) Rice Crispies

Bliss Balls

Melt the butter or margarine and mix with sugar and milk. Add dry ingredients and vanilla essence, mix well, roll into balls and dip in the coconut. Place in refrigerator to set.

MAKES 12-14 BALLS.

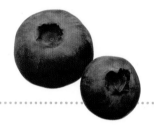

125 g (4 oz) butter OR margarine
6 tbs sugar
5 tbs milk
12 tbs milk powder
3 tbs cocoa powder OR drinking chocolate
125 g (4 oz) sultanas
½ tsp vanilla essence
desiccated coconut, for coating

Chocolate Nuts and Dried Fruit

Melt the chocolate in a bowl over hot water. Dip the dried fruit and nuts into the chocolate, one piece at a time, and place on an oiled baking tray. Put the tray in the refrigerator to harden the chocolate. Store in a tin.

500 g (1 lb) cooking chocolate, plain or milk
60 g (2 oz) dried mango slices
60 g (2 oz) dried apricots
60 g (2 oz) large currants
60 g (2 oz) large sultanas
60 g (2 oz) whole almonds, blanched
60 g (2 oz) Brazil nuts
60 g (2 oz) hazelnuts

Chocolate Spread

Place all the ingredients in a saucepan over a low heat. Stir continuously until everything is melted and blended. Leave to cool before transferring to a jar for storing.

2 tbs cocoa powder
125 g (4 oz) butter OR margarine
125 g (4 oz) golden syrup

Chocolate Truffles

With a rolling pin, crush the biscuits to a fine powder and put into a bowl. Add syrup and water. Melt the butter or margarine and chocolate. Add to biscuits and mix well. Stir in the almond essence. Divide mixture into small balls and roll them in the chocolate vermicelli.

MAKES 6-8 TRUFFLES.

125 g (4 oz) sweet biscuits
1 tbs golden syrup
1 tbs hot water
30 g (1 oz) butter OR margarine
60 g (2 oz) chocolate, melted
1 tsp almond essence
chocolate vermicelli (chocolate sprinkles), for coating

Coconut Ice

Mix the coconut, condensed milk and vanilla essence in a bowl with a wooden spoon to make a stiff dough. Add more coconut if the mixture is very moist. Grease a baking sheet and spread the mixture evenly on it. Leave in refrigerator for 2-3 hours or until it hardens. Sprinkle icing sugar on top and cut into pieces.

MAKES 18-20.

350 g (12 oz) desiccated coconut
400 g (13 oz) sweetened condensed milk
1 tsp vanilla essence
300 g (10 oz) icing sugar

Coconut Pyramids

Set the oven to 160°C/325°F/Gas Mark 3. Combine all the ingredients. Divide the mixture into 13 little balls and shape into cones. Bake for 10 minutes.

MAKES 13 PYRAMIDS.

250 g (8 oz) desiccated coconut
1 tsp vanilla essence
5 tbs condensed milk

Coconut Squares (Opposite)

Put the sugar and water in a pan and bring to boil. Simmer for one minute; add all the ingredients (except the almonds and pistachios) and cook on low heat, stirring continuously with a flat metal or wooden spoon. Continue to cook until the mixture does not stick to the hands when touched. Remove from heat. Meanwhile, grease a shallow 8 inch tray with a little butter or oil, place the coconut mixture in it and roll out or press the mixture to cover the tray evenly. Sprinkle the nuts over this and press lightly into the rolled mixture. Allow to cool until firmly set. Cut into squares.

Note – This will keep for a few days only. You may keep them in fridge to keep them fresh for longer time. They can be frozen if desired. If frozen, then allow them to defrost at room temperature before serving.

MAKES 10-12 SQUARES.

250 g (8 oz) sugar
125 ml (4 fl oz) water
325 g (10 oz) fine desiccated coconut
100 g (3.5 oz) milk powder – full cream
¼ pack block coconut, grated
¼ tsp ground cardamom
3-4 drops of food colouring (optional)
finely sliced or chopped almonds and
*   pistachios for decoration*

Coffee and Chocolate Truffles

Mix coffee and water and allow to cool. Put syrup, cocoa, butter or margarine and cream into a pan. Stir over a low heat until well mixed and then bring to the boil. Remove from the heat, add coffee liquid and stir in the sugar. Beat until smooth and allow to cool. Roll the mixture into balls. Roll each ball in the cocoa powder, place in an airtight tin and store in the refrigerator.

MAKES 20 TRUFFLES.

4 tbs instant coffee granules
1 tbs hot water
1½ tbs golden syrup
60 g (2 oz) cocoa
60 g (2 oz) butter OR margarine
2 tbs double cream
150 g (5 oz) icing sugar
Cocoa powder, for coating

Easy Fudge

In a saucepan, heat together butter or margarine and water. Stir until the butter or margarine has melted and then bring to the boil. Sift together sugar, milk powder and cocoa powder. Add the butter or margarine and stir until well combined. Add nuts and turn onto a greased baking tin 20 x 20 x 5 cm (8 x 8 x 2 in). Cover and chill for several hours or till firm. Cut into squares.

MAKES 750 G (1½ LB) OF FUDGE.

60 g (2 oz) butter OR margarine
80 ml (2½ fl oz) water
500 g (1 lb) icing sugar
60 g (2 oz) non fat dry milk powder
60 g (2 oz) unsweetened cocoa powder
60 g (2 oz) nuts, chopped

Gulab Jamun (Opposite)

Mix all the ingredients for the syrup in a large pan and bring to the boil. Lower the heat and simmer for 30 minutes. The syrup is now ready.

Put aside to cool to room temperature.

To prepare the dough for the Jamuns, add the ground cardamom and saffron to the milk and bring to the boil. Take the pan off the heat and stir in the evaporated milk. Mix the milk powder, plain flour, bicarbonate of soda and 3 teaspoons of oil in a large bowl.
Slowly add the milk mixture and knead into a soft smooth dough.

Make small smooth balls (either round or oval shaped) about 18 mm (¾ inch) in diameter.

Heat the oil mixed with 3 tablespoons of ghee and fry the Jamuns, few at a time, on an extremely low heat until they puff up into a fairly big size.

Once risen and expanded, turn the heat up slightly and fry until dark brown.

Drain the Jamuns on a kitchen towel and leave aside for 2 minutes.

Add the Jamuns to the cooled syrup and soak for 2-3 hours before serving.

MAKES 40 GULAB JAMUNS.

SYRUP
500 g (1 lb) sugar
500 ml (16 fl oz) water
½ tsp cardamom, freshly ground
a few strands of saffron

JAMUNS
¼ tsp cardamom seeds, freshly ground
a few strands of saffron
125 ml (4 fl oz) milk
210 ml (7 fl oz) evaporated milk
210 g (7oz) milk powder
105 g (3½ oz) plain flour
¼ tsp bicarbonate of soda
3 tsp oil
3 tbs ghee (clarified butter)
oil, for deep frying

Nut Crunch

Moisten the rolling pin with oil. Place sugar, oil and lemon juice in a pan and stir over a low heat. Stir continuously and within 5 minutes the sugar will turn to a smooth light brown liquid. As soon as this happens, remove from the heat immediately. Very quickly add the nuts or whatever you have chosen. If necessary add more nuts until you reach the desired consistency. All this must be done very quickly. Place on an oiled board and roll flat with a rolling pin. Let it cool for 10 minutes then cut into squares.

To store: place cellophane paper between the layers to avoid sticking and store in an airtight container.

MAKES 25 PIECES.

45 g (1½ oz) sugar
1 tbs oil
2 drops of lemon juice
150 g (5 oz) chopped nuts
OR sesame seeds
OR dried sliced coconut
OR roasted chick peas

Date Fingers

Combine flour and muesli. Rub in the butter or margarine and at in the sugar. Combine the dates, lemon juice and water in a saucepan and cook over a low heat until soft. Press half the crumble mixture into a greased 18 cm (7 in) square baking tin. Spread with the date mixture and press the remaining crumble mixture on top.

Bake at 180°C/350°F/Gas Mark 4 for 30 minutes.

MAKES 25 FINGERS.

CRUMBLE
125 g (4 oz) self-raising flour
125 g (4 oz) muesli
125 g (4 oz) butter OR margarine
60 g (2 oz) brown sugar

FILLING
250 g (8 oz) dates, chopped
2 tbs lemon juice
3 tbs water

Peppermint Cream

Mix icing sugar to a stiff paste with single cream. Add peppermint essence. Knead until quite smooth, adding more icing sugar or milk, if necessary, to make a paste which can be rolled out. Roll out to 6 mm (¼ inch) thick and cut into rounds or whatever shapes you desire. Place on greaseproof paper to set.

250 g (8 oz) icing sugar
2 tbs single cream
½ tsp peppermint essence

Ice Lollies

Mix the ingredients in a jug and pour into ice-cube or ice-lolly moulds. Leave in the freezer until solid.

MAKES 6 LOLLIES.

250 ml (8 fl oz) orange squash
1-2 tsp lemon juice
1 tsp caster sugar

Toffee (Opposite)

Melt the butter or margarine and sugar in a saucepan. Add condensed milk and syrup. Allow to boil slowly for 20 minutes, stirring all the time. Toffee can be tested by dropping a little in water—if it hardens, it is ready. Before removing from the heat, add vanilla essence. Pour the mixture on a well-greased tray and spread evenly.

90 g (3 oz) butter OR margarine
150 g (5 oz) sugar
400 g (13 oz) sweetened condensed milk
1 tbs golden syrup
¼ tsp vanilla essence

Cut into squares when cool.

MAKES 30-40 TOFFEES.

Toffee Apples

Wash and dry the apples. Put sugar, water and lemon juice into a saucepan and bring to the boil until the sugar dissolves and mixture becomes pale brown in colour. Remove the saucepan from the heat.

4 eating apples
250 g (8 oz) white sugar
45 ml (1½ fl oz) water
3 tbs lemon juice

Use a fork to skewer the top of each apple and dip the apple into the syrup, making sure it is completely covered.

Leave in a cool place for the syrup to harden.

MAKES 4 TOFFEE APPLES.

Breads, Pastry, Buns & Scones

Bhatura (Opposite)

Mix the flour, salt, sugar, yeast and oil in a bowl. Add yoghurt and enough water to make into a soft manageable dough. Cover the dough and leave in a warm place for 1-2 hours to rise until double the size. Knead the dough and divide into 6-8 portions. Roll out each portion on a floured surface into 13 cm (5 in) diameter rounds.

Heat the oil in a wok. Place the rounds into the hot oil—the bhatura will puff up. Fry on both sides until golden brown. Remove with a slotted spoon and place on paper towel to absorb the excess oil.

Serve hot with Chick Pea Curry (Channa) (page 53).

MAKES 6-8 BHATURAS.

360 g (12 oz) plain flour
1 tsp salt
1 tbs sugar
1 level tsp instant dried yeast
2 tbs oil
60 ml (2 fl oz) plain yoghurt
lukewarm water
oil, for frying

Bread Rolls

Mix all the dry ingredients together. Add the water a little at a time to form a soft dough. Knead the dough for 5 minutes or until elastic. Make into small rolls, place well apart on a greased baking tray, and allow them to rise until double in size. Once risen, bake in a hot oven at 200°C/400°F/Gas Mark 6 for 20-25 minutes. Brush baked rolls with a little oil while hot and allow to cool.

MAKES 10-12 ROLLS.

500 g (1 lb) strong plain flour
1 tsp salt
1 tbs instant dried yeast
lukewarm water
2 tbs oil

Brown Bread

Mix the flour and salt in a large bowl. Add sugar and yeast and rub in the butter or margarine. Slowly add lukewarm water, mix together to bind into a soft dough. Knead the dough for 5 minutes or until elastic. Cover and leave in a warm place to rise for 1- 2 hours. Grease a 1 lb loaf tin. Knead the dough well and press into the loaf tin. Allow it to rise in a warm place until doubled in size. Once risen, bake in a hot oven at 180°C/350°F/Gas Mark 4 for 25-30 minutes. Brush with oil and cool on the rack.

MAKES 1 LOAF.

500 g (1 lb) strong wholemeal bread
   flour
1 tsp salt
1-2 tbs sugar
30 g (1 oz) instant yeast
30 g (1 oz) butter OR margarine
lukewarm water

Celery Rolls

Mix together all the dry dough ingredients and the oil. Add the water a little at a time to form a soft dough. Knead the dough for 5 minutes or until elastic. Cover and leave in a warm place to rise for 1-2 hours.

Heat the oil in a pan, add the tomato purée, salt and paprika and cook until the oil has blended into the purée. Leave aside.

Roll out the dough into rectangle 5 mm (¼ in) thick and spread the tomato paste evenly all over the dough. Sprinkle cheese and celery evenly over the dough and roll the dough into a Swiss roll. With a knife, cut the rolled dough into 1 cm (½ in) thick slices and place them on a greased baking tray, with enough space around them to rise to twice the size. Bake in pre-heated oven at 200°C/400°F/Gas Mark 6 for 20 minutes until brown.

To prepare the topping, heat more oil in a small saucepan, add the mustard seeds until they pop, then add the sesame seeds and remove from the heat. Spread this over each roll with a teaspoon and sprinkle coriander or parsley on top.

MAKES 8-10 ROLLS.

DOUGH
500 g (1 lb) strong plain flour
1 tsp salt
1 tbs instant dried yeast
2 tbs oil
lukewarm water

FILLING
185 g (6 oz) tomato purée
2 tbs oil
2 tsp salt
1 tsp paprika
125 g (4 oz) Cheddar cheese, grated
250 g (8 oz) celery, finely chopped

TOPPING
2 tbs oil
1 tsp mustard seeds
2-3 tbs sesame seeds
30 g (1 oz) fresh coriander OR parsley

Cheese Loaf

Heat liquid and oil until lukewarm. Combine flour, yeast, salt and cheese in a large bowl. Add liquid and mix together to form the dough. Knead for 10 minutes, place in a bowl and cover with a damp cloth. Leave in a warm area to rise for 1 hour. Knead again for 10 minutes until the dough is smooth and elastic. Place in a 1 kg (2 lb) loaf tin, cover with a damp cloth and leave to prove in a warm place for 30-40 minutes.

Bake in a hot oven at 220°C/425°F/Gas Mark 7 for 15 minutes, then lower the temperature to 190°C/375°F/Gas Mark 5 for a further 20-25 minutes, until the bread sounds hollow when tapped. Turn onto a wire rack.

The amount of liquid varies according to the type of flour used. Wholegrain flours need more liquid.

MAKES 1 LOAF.

600 ml (1 pint) water OR milk OR half water, half milk
1 tbs oil
500 g (1 lb) bread flour
1 tbs instant dried yeast
¼ tsp salt
60 g (2 oz) strong Cheddar cheese, grated

Chapatis

Put flour in a bowl and rub in the oil. Make a soft dough by adding enough water, a little at a time. Knead for a few minutes, cover and leave aside for 1 hour.

Place an iron griddle or heavy flat pan on a medium heat. Knead the dough with oiled hands and divide into 20 small portions. Make into balls using the palms of your hands. Flatten the balls and roll out on floured surface into rounds 18 cm (7 in) in diameter.

Place one rolled chapati on the hot griddle or pan. Cook lightly one side, turn after 20-30 seconds and cook the other side. Turn frequently so it doesn't burn. Remove from the pan when puffed up, place on a paper towel on a plate, and lightly spread with butter or margarine.

MAKES 20 CHAPATIS.

360 g (12 oz) chapati flour
1-2 tbs oil
warm water
butter OR margarine

Cheese Rolls

Make the dough as for Cheese Loaf (opposite) and after it has risen the first time, divide it into 10 equal pieces. Knead each piece into a ball press into a small circle and place a teaspoon of Cottage Cheese in centre of each circle. Bring both sides of the circle together to seal the cheese completely. Pinch the dough together to form a tight seal. Make sure the cheese is completely sealed in. Place onto a floured baking tray. Cover and leave to rise until doubled in size.

Bake in a hot oven at 220°C/425°F/Gas Mark 7 for 10-15 minutes or until golden brown

MAKES 10 ROLLS.

Cheese (page 212) 5 tbs Cottage

Corn Bread

Sift the dry ingredients together in a bowl. Combine milk, oil and molasses in a jug and pour onto the dry ingredients. Mix well and place the dough in well-greased loaf tin.

Bake at 220°C/425°F/Gas Mark 7 for about 20-30 minutes.

Masa Harina: a corn flour used to make tortillas, available in the baking or Mexican food section of most grocery stores.

SERVES 6.

180 ml (6 fl oz) milk
90 ml (3 fl oz) oil
3 tbs molasses
90 g (3 oz) cornmeal
8 g (¼ oz) masa harina
30 g (1 oz) plain flour
2 tsp baking powder
2 tbs sugar
1 tsp salt

Focaccia (Opposite)

Sift the flour and salt into a fairly large bowl. Add the oil and yeast and mix well. Add enough water to form a soft dough. Cover and leave in a warm place to rise. When it has risen, knead the dough again for a couple of minutes and roll it out to 2.5 cm (1 in) thick. Grease a flat baking tray, and place the rolled dough on it. Press fingertips lightly into the dough. Brush with olive oil and sprinkle with oregano/rosemary.

Bake in a hot oven at 200°C/400°F/Gas Mark 6 for 20 minutes or until top is golden.

Variations: olives and sun dried tomatoes can be mixed into the flour.

MAKES 1 LOAF.

500 g (1 lb) bread flour
1 tsp salt
6 tbs oil
30 g (1 oz) instant dried yeast
360 ml (12 fl oz) lukewarm water,
 to mix
60 g (2 oz) oregano/rosemary for
 topping
oil, for topping
salt, for topping

Granary Bread

Mix flour, salt, sugar and yeast in a bowl. Melt the butter or margarine in a saucepan and rub into the flour. Add water to form a soft dough. Knead the dough well, cover with a tea towel and leave in a warm place to rise for 45 minutes to 1 hour. Knead again for 5 minutes and place in a greased bread tin. Cover with a tea towel and allow to rise again.

Bake in the centre of a hot oven at 190°C / 375°F / Gas Mark 5 for 35-40 minutes. Cool on a wire rack.

MAKES 1 LOAF.

60 g (2 oz) butter OR margarine
500 g (1 lb) granary flour
1 tsp salt
2 tbs brown sugar
30 g (1 oz) instant dried yeast
lukewarm water

Naan Bread

Place flour, salt, sugar and yeast in a large bowl, add oil and mix together. Add yoghurt and enough water to make a soft dough. Cover the dough with a tea cloth and leave in a warm place to rise until double the size. Knead the dough and divide it into 8 balls. Dip in dry flour and roll out each ball into an oval shape on a floured surface. Heat an iron griddle or a frying pan and cook like a chapatti until golden brown on both sides.

Serve with any vegetable curry.

MAKES 8 NAANS.

500 g (1 lb) plain flour
1½ tsp salt
2 tsp sugar
1½ level tsp instant dried yeast
120 ml (4 oz) plain yoghurt
lukewarm water
60 g (2 fl oz) oil
plain flour, for rolling out

Toast Sticks

Mix butter or margarine, sugar, bicarbonate of soda, custard powder and food colouring until soft and fluffy. Add milk, flour, salt and fennel seeds and form into a soft dough. Take small portions of dough and roll between the palm of your hands into long sticks, arrange on a baking sheet and bake at 180°C/350°F/Gas Mark 4 for 25-30 minutes.

MAKES 12-15 STICKS.

60 g (2 oz) butter OR margarine
3 tsp sugar
pinch of bicarbonate of soda
2 tsp custard powder
2 drops of yellow food colouring
*   (optional)*
2-3 tbs milk
250 g (8 oz) plain flour
1 tsp salt
8 g (¼ oz) fennel seeds

White Bread

Sift flour and salt into a large bowl, add sugar and yeast. Mix in the oil and add the water slowly to form soft and elastic dough. Cover and leave in a warm place to rise for 1-2 hours. Grease a 500 g (1 lb) loaf tin. Knead the dough for 5-10 minutes and place in the tin. Leave to rise again. Once risen, bake in a hot oven at 180°C/350°F/Gas Mark 4 for 25-30 minutes.

This recipe can be used to make 12-15 bread rolls.

MAKES 1 LOAF OR 12-15 ROLLS.

500 g (1 lb) strong white bread flour
1 tsp salt
2 tbs oil
1-2 tsp sugar
30 g (1 oz) dried instant yeast
lukewarm water

Pitta Bread (Opposite)

Sift the flour, and salt into a fairly large mixing bowl. Mix in the yeast and sugar. Add in the oil and lukewarm water to the dry ingredients to form the dough. Knead well for 5-7 minutes. Cover and leave in a warm place for 1-2 hours to rise. Turn onto a floured surface, knead well and divide into 10-12 portions, depending on the size required. Roll out each portion into a circle and place on a baking sheet and cover with a cloth. Let pittas rise for 20-30 minutes. Cook in a pre-heated oven 220°C / 428°F / Gas Mark 7 for 4-5 minutes until puffed and both sides become brown.

500 g (1 lb) white bread flour
1 tsp salt
30 g (1 oz) instant dried yeast
1½ tbs sugar
1-2 tsp vegetable oil
lukewarm water, to mix

Pitta breads are ideal for filling with a salad.

MAKES 10-12 PITTA BREADS.

Puris

Mix the flour and oil together in a bowl. Pour in the water little by little to make a smooth, firm dough. Knead it for 3-5 minutes and leave it to stand for ½ hour.

500 g (1 lb) chapati flour
2-3 tbs oil
lukewarm water
oil, for frying

Heat the oil in a deep frying pan or a wok. Knead the dough again and make small round balls, the size of a walnut. Roll each ball to about 7.5 cm (3 in) in diameter and fry in the hot oil. Puris should puff up like a ball. Turn them gently onto the other side and cook for 30 seconds. Place on a paper towel to remove any excess oil.

Can be served hot or cold.

MAKES 30 PURIS.

Shortbread Pastry

Put the flour, sugar and salt into a bowl. Rub the butter into the flour with the fingertips until the mixture resembles fine breadcrumbs. Add sufficient cold water to form a fairly soft dough, taking care to handle it as little as possible. Leave to rest in the refrigerator for at least 30 minutes.

Roll out to 1 cm (½ in) thick on a well floured surface and fit in a baking tray. Prick the base with a fork and top with a filling of your choice.

Bake at 200°C/400°F/Gas Mark 6 for 20 minutes.

500 g (16 oz) self raising flour
90 g (3 oz) sugar
360 g (12 oz) butter
1½ tsp salt
5-6 tbs cold water

Shortcrust Pastry

Sift the flour and salt into a bowl. Add butter cut into small pieces or margarine. Rub the butter or margarine into the flour with the fingertips until the mixture resembles fine breadcrumbs. Add water and knead the mixture into a pliable dough.

Allow to rest in the refrigerator for at least 30 minutes.

Roll out on a well floured surface and use to line a pie dish, put in a filling of your choice and cook at 200°C/400°F/Gas Mark 6 for 20 minutes.

ENOUGH FOR TWO 25 CM (10 IN) PIES.

1 kg (2 lb) plain flour
1 tsp salt
500 g (1 lb) butter OR margarine
180 ml (6 fl oz) cold water

Pie Pastry

Sift the flour into a bowl. Add sugar, rub butter or margarine into the flour until the mixture resembles fine breadcrumbs. Add water to form a firm dough. Handle as little as possible to keep it light. Allow to rest in the refrigerator for at least 30 minutes.

Roll out on a well floured surface and use this to line a pie dish, put in a filling of your choice and cook at 200°C/400°F/Gas Mark 6 for 20 minutes.

ENOUGH FOR TWO 25 CM (10 IN) PIES.

500 g (1 lb) plain flour
60 g (2 oz) caster sugar
350 g (11 oz) butter OR margarine
3 tbs cold water

Chocolate Buns (Opposite)

Sift flour, custard powder and salt into a large bowl. Add the yeast and sugar and mix. Pour milk slowly into the flour to form a soft dough. Cover the bowl and leave in a warm place for 1 hour to rise. Knead the dough for 2-3 minutes, divide it into 14-16 small balls. Place them on a greased baking tray, spacing them well apart and cover with a tea cloth. Put in a warm place until they have risen to twice the size. Bake in a hot oven at 200°C/400°F/Gas Mark 6 for 10-13 minutes until golden brown. Remove and place on a wire rack to cool.

Break the cooking chocolate into small pieces and put in a glass bowl. To melt the chocolate, place the bowl over hot water or microwave for 2 minutes. Dip just the top half of the cooled buns into the chocolate. Leave aside for the chocolate to set.

MAKES 14-16 BUNS.

500 g (1 lb) plain flour
2 tbs custard powder
pinch of salt
30 g (1 oz) dried instant yeast
4 tbs sugar
600 ml (1 pint) lukewarm milk
400 g (13 oz) cooking chocolate

Crumpets

Sift the flour and salt into a bowl. Add yeast and sugar and mix together. Add lukewarm milk to the flour and mix thoroughly until a smooth batter is formed. Cover the bowl with a cloth and leave to stand for 1 hour. Grease a frying pan, placing crumpet rings or round pastry cutters on it. When the pan is hot, pour 2-3 tablespoon of batter into each ring. Allow to cook for a couple of minutes until small holes appear on the surface and the batter has dried out. Lift off the rings and turn the crumpets over gently. Cook them until golden brown on both sides.

MAKES 12-14 CRUMPETS.

500 g (1 lb) plain flour
1½ tsp salt
2 tbs dried instant yeast
30 g (1 oz) sugar
750 ml (1¼ pints) milk, lukewarm
oil, for frying

Jam Buns

Sift flour, baking powder and salt in a bowl. Rub the butter or margarine into the flour until the mixture resembles fine breadcrumbs. Add the sugar and milk. Mix to make a stiff dough. Turn out onto a floured board and knead lightly. Divide into 10-12 pieces. Make an indent in the middle of each bun and put in ½ teaspoon of jam. Bake at 220°C/425°F/Gas Mark 7 for 20 minutes.

Makes 10-12 buns.

250 g (8 oz) self-raising flour
pinch of salt
1 level tsp baking powder
90 g (3 oz) butter OR margarine
125 g (4 oz) sugar
125 ml (4 fl oz) milk
5-6 tsp jam

Doughnuts (Opposite)

Mix together flour, dried yeast, sugar and salt. Add oil and rub in well. Gradually add sufficient water to make a firm dough. Knead for about 10 minutes or until smooth. Roll out the dough ½ inch thick and cut using a round pastry cutter and form the hole in the middle with your fingers. For oblong doughnuts, divide into 16 pieces and roll into shape. Place doughnuts well apart on an oiled baking tray, and leave in a warm place to rise until double in size. Deep fry over a medium heat for 2 minutes on each side or until golden brown. Dip in a mixture of caster sugar and cinnamon whilst still hot.

MAKES ABOUT 16 DOUGHNUTS.

625 g (1 ¼ lb) white plain flour
30 g (1 oz) instant dried yeast
4 tbs sugar
1½ tsp salt
3 tbs oil
luke warm water
1.2 l (2 pints) oil, for frying
caster sugar, for dusting
pinch of ground cinnamon, for dusting

Hot Cross Buns

Set the oven to 220°C/425°F/Gas Mark 7. Sift the flour and salt into a large bowl. Add sugar and yeast, rub in the butter or margarine and add all the spices and fruits. Mix together and add the water slowly to form a soft elastic dough. Cover and leave in a warm place to rise for 1-2 hours.

Punch down the dough. Divide it into 12-14 pieces, form into smooth balls, and place them 2.5 cm (1 in) apart on a greased baking tray. Cover and leave in a warm place for 30 minutes or until well risen. Bake for 20 minutes. Meanwhile prepare the glazing by heating the sugar and water until the sugar is dissolved, and brush the tops of the buns with it as soon as they come out of the oven. Cool on a wire rack.

Mix the icing sugar and lemon juice to a paste consistency and make crosses over the buns using an icing bag.

MAKES 12-14 BUNS.

DOUGH
500 g (1 lb) strong white bread flour
1 tsp salt
1-2 tbs sugar
30 g (1 oz) dried instant yeast
30 g (1 oz) butter OR margarine
½ tsp mixed spice
½ tsp cinnamon, ground
½ tsp nutmeg, grated
90 g (3 oz) currants OR sultanas
lukewarm water

GLAZING
30 g (1 oz) sugar
2 tbs water

ICING
90 g (3 oz) icing sugar
1 tsp lemon juice

Apple Scones

Sift together the flour, salt and baking powder. Rub in the butter or margarine. Add the sugar, grated apple and enough milk to make a soft, but not sticky, dough. Turn the mixture onto a floured surface and knead lightly. Roll out into a 20 cm (8 in) round and place on a greased and floured baking tray. Mark the scone into 8 equal pieces. Brush all over the top with milk and sprinkle with demerara sugar if desired.

Bake at 200°C/400°F/Gas Mark 6 for 20-25 minutes or until well risen and golden brown. Remove from the oven and cool for 10 minutes.

MAKES 8 SCONES.

250 g (8 oz) plain flour
½ tsp salt
2 tsp baking powder
60 g (2 oz) butter OR margarine
60 g (2 oz) caster sugar
1 medium size cooking apple, grated
4 tbs milk
milk, for topping
demerara sugar, for topping
  (optional)

Apricot Scones

Grease and flour two 18 cm (7 in) sandwich tins. Mix all the ingredients thoroughly in a bowl except the milk. Add enough milk to make a soft dough. Divide in half. Roll out each half to about 2.5 cm (1 in) thick and cut 7 scones from each half. Place 7 scones in each sandwich tin, 6 around the edge and one in the middle.

Bake at 200°C/400°F/Gas Mark 6 for 20 minutes.

MAKES 14 SCONES.

500 g (1 lb) self-raising flour
2 tsp salt
30 g (1 oz) caster sugar
300 g (10 oz) butter OR margarine
rind of 1 orange, grated
60 g (2 oz) dried apricots, soaked
and chopped
60 g (2 oz) raisins
250 ml (8 fl oz) milk

Banana Scones

Put the flour, baking powder and sugar into a mixing bowl. Rub in the butter or margarine. Stir in mashed banana and add enough water into the flour mixture to form into a soft dough. Knead lightly. Turn the mixture onto a lightly floured surface. Roll out to 2.5 cm (1 in) thick. With a 5 cm (2 in) pastry cutter, stamp out 18 scones. Place scones on greased and floured baking sheets, brush with a little milk and sprinkle with demerara sugar if desired.

Bake at 200°C/400°F/Gas Mark 6 for 15 minutes or until golden brown and firm to touch. Cool on a wire rack.

MAKES 18 SCONES.

250 g (8 oz) plain flour
2 tsp baking powder
60 g (2 oz) caster sugar
90 g (3 oz) butter OR margarine
250 g (8 oz) banana, mashed
water
milk, for topping
2 tbs demerara sugar (optional)

Cheese Scones

Place flour and salt in a bowl. Rub butter or margarine into the flour until the mixture resembles fine breadcrumbs. Add the cheese and enough milk and water to make a soft dough. Turn out onto a lightly floured surface and roll out thickly. With a 5 cm (2 in) pastry cutter, stamp out 10-12 scones. Arrange on the tray, brush the tops with a little milk and bake at 200°C/400°F/Gas Mark 6 for 10-15 minutes or until well risen and golden brown. Cool on a wire rack.

Serve with cream, cream cheese or jam.

MAKES 10-12 SCONES.

250 g (8 oz) self-raising flour
pinch of salt
60 g (2 oz) butter OR margarine
90 g (3 oz) mild Cheddar cheese,
  grated
150 ml (¼ pint) milk and water
  mixed

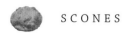

Fruit Scones

Sift flour, baking powder and sugar. Cut the butter or margarine into small pieces and rub into the flour until the mixture resembles breadcrumbs. Add sultanas. Pour in milk and mix to form a soft dough. Turn out onto a lightly floured surface and roll out thickly. With a 5 cm (2 in) pastry cutter, stamp out 10-12 scones.

Bake at 200°C/400°F/Gas Mark 6 for 12-15 minutes until golden brown.

Standard Scone Mix is butter rubbed into flour and a pinch of salt.

MAKES 10-12 SCONES.

250 g (8 oz) self-raising flour
1 tsp baking powder
30 g (1 oz) caster sugar
60 g (2 oz) butter OR margarine
125 g (4 oz) sultanas
7 tbs milk

Parsley Scones

Mix thoroughly all ingredients except 30 g (1 oz) of cheese and the milk. Add enough milk to mix to a soft dough. Cut dough in half and shape each half into a 15 cm (6 in) round. Place on two floured baking sheets. Mark each round into 6 wedges, cutting nearly halfway through the dough. Brush the tops with milk and sprinkle the remaining cheese over.

Bake at 200°C/400°F/Gas Mark 6 for 20 minutes.

MAKES 12 SCONES.

500 g (1 lb) self-raising flour
¼ tsp cayenne pepper
2 tbs fresh parsley, chopped
300 g (10 oz) butter OR margarine
pinch of salt
220 g (7 oz) mature Cheddar cheese, grated
250 ml (8 fl oz) milk
milk, for glazing

Potato Scones

Set oven to 200°C/400°F/Gas Mark 6. Sift flour, baking powder and salt into a bowl and mix with butter or margarine and potatoes. Add sufficient milk to form a soft dough. Turn out onto a floured surface and knead lightly. Roll out to 1 cm (½ in) thick and cut into small triangles. Place the scones on a floured baking sheet. Brush each scone with milk.

Bake for 10-15 minutes until golden brown.

MAKES 6-8 SCONES.

250 g (8 oz) self-raising flour
1 tsp baking powder
¼ tsp salt
60 g (2 oz) butter OR margarine
60 g (2 oz) potatoes, boiled, peeled and mashed
4 tbs milk

Yoghurt Scones

Set the oven to 200°C/400°F/Gas Mark 6. Sift flour, salt and baking powder into a bowl. Rub in the butter or margarine until the mixture resembles breadcrumbs, then stir in the sugar. Add yoghurt and mix to a soft dough. Knead very gently on a floured surface and roll out to 1 cm (½ in) thick. Cut into small rounds with a cutter and place on floured baking sheets. Bake for 12-15 minutes until golden brown. Cool on a wire rack.

For best results, don't handle the dough too much.

Variation: add 1 teaspoon of dry mustard and a pinch of cayenne pepper to the dry ingredients. Replace the sugar with 90 g (3 oz) grated cheese and 1 tablespoon of sesame seeds.

Eat them on the day they are made.

MAKES 12-15 SCONES.

250 g (8 oz) wholemeal flour
½ tsp salt
2 level tsp baking powder
60 g (2 oz) butter OR margarine
1 tbs muscovado sugar
150 ml (¼ pint) plain yoghurt

Drinks

Banana Milk Shake (Opposite)

Liquidise all the ingredients in a blender and serve chilled.

SERVES 1-2.

1 banana, sliced
500 ml (½ pint) milk
1 tbs honey OR sugar

Coconut and Banana Smoothie

Blend all the ingredients, except the coconut, in a blender for about 1 minute. Pour into a glass and sprinkle the coconut on top.

SERVES 3-4.

250 ml (8 oz) plain yoghurt
125 ml (4 fl oz) milk
1 banana, sliced
1 tsp honey
2-3 drops vanilla essence
1 tsp desiccated coconut

Elderflower Cordial

Pour all the ingredients into a very large mixing bowl. Stir until the sugar is dissolved. Leave for 24 hours, then strain carefully. The cordial can be frozen. Ice cube bags are ideal as 1 cube is enough for a tumbler of drink. To drink, dilute to taste with water.

SERVES 6-8.

25 elderflower heads
60 g (2 oz) citric acid
2 chopped lemons
1 kg (2 lb) caster sugar
1.2 l (2 pints) boiling water

Fresh Lemonade

Peel lemon finely and squeeze out the juice. Dissolve honey or sugar in water, add lemon peel and let stand for 30 minutes. Then add the lemon juice. Chill. Strain before serving.

SERVES 4-6.

1 lemon
honey OR sugar to taste
600 ml (1 pint) boiling water

Fruit and Vegetable Drink

Liquidise the juices and cucumber together in a blender. Decorate with mint.

SERVES 6-8.

125 ml (4 fl oz) carrot juice
125 ml (4 fl oz) orange juice
250 ml (8 fl oz) apple juice
¼ cucumber, peeled
mint, for decoration

Fruit Cocktail

Mix all the juices. Add lime to taste. Garnish with small chunks of fresh fruit. Serve chilled.

Suggested fruits for garnishing are pineapple, nectarine, peach, orange, kiwi.

SERVES 15-20.

600 ml (1 pint) red grape juice
600 ml (1 pint) pineapple juice
1.8 L (3 pints) orange juice
limes, freshly squeezed
fresh fruit, for garnish

Pineapple Nectar

Place yoghurt, pineapple juice and honey or sugar in a blender and blend. Serve chilled, decorated with fresh pineapple cubes and sprinkled with coconut.

SERVES 6.

125 ml (4 oz) plain yoghurt
125 ml (4 fl oz) pineapple juice
1 tbs honey OR sugar
fresh pineapple, cubed for decoration
desiccated coconut, for decoration

Mango Milk Shake (Opposite)

Place all the ingredients in a blender and blend until soft and creamy. Serve chilled.

Variation: Strawberry Milk Shake can be made using 250 g (8 oz) of strawberries instead of mangoes and 1-2 teaspoons of sugar.

SERVES 4.

600 ml (1 pint) milk
2 large ripe mangoes, peeled and chopped
1 tsp sugar

Jams, Cheese & Yoghurt

Tips for preparing and preserving jams

1) Fruits

Fresh, dry and not over-ripe.

2) Sugar

Preserving OR granulated sugar.

3) Proportion

1 part of Fruit to 1 part of Sugar.

4) Cooking

Use a preserving pan (a thick-based saucepan) and fill no more than two-thirds. Use a wooden spoon to stir jam. Sugar must not be allowed to boil until it has dissolved.

5) To Test For Setting Point

When the jam has been boiling for 5 minutes, remove the pan from the heat and spoon a little onto an ice-cold saucer. Leave in the refrigerator until cold. If the surface of the jam frills and wrinkles when pushed with the finger, the jam is at setting point. If not, return the pan to the heat and boil for a further 3-5 minutes. Test again as before. Repeat until setting point is reached.

6) Jars

Clean, dry, steralized glass or earthenware jars should be used.

7) Covering And Labelling

It can be done immediately, or when the jam is cold (in which case a teaspoon of vinegar on top will stop the jam from going mouldy). Use wax tissue or cellophane paper.

Date Spread

Remove any stones or stems from the dates, and chop them. Cook the dates gently with water in a saucepan until soft. Add the lemon juice. After cooking, allow it to cool. Store in a jar in the refrigerator.

250 g (8 oz) dates
300 ml (½ pint) water
1 tsp lemon juice

Mincemeat—Sugarless

Stir all the ingredients together well. Mix at least a day before needed, and stir from time to time.

This mincemeat should not be kept for more than a week, as it contains no sugar.

250 g (8 oz) currants
125 g (4 oz) seeded raisins, chopped
125 g (4 oz) sultanas
375 g (12 oz) Bramley apples, unpeeled, cored and grated
1 tsp orange peel, grated
1 tsp mixed spice
3 tbs lemon juice
2 tbs oil

Mincemeat—Preserve

Wash the dried fruit. Mix the mixed spice and lemon rind with the sugar. Add the dried fruit, lemon juice, fat or oil, apples and mixed peel. Stir well. Allow to stand for at least one day before use, stirring from time to time. Keep covered to prevent drying out.

This mincemeat can be put in jars and will keep for weeks.

MAKES AT LEAST 72 MINCE PIES.

250 g (8 oz) currants
250 g (8 oz) sultanas
1¼ tsp mixed spice
juice and rind of 1 lemon
500 g (1 lb) sugar
180 g (6 oz) vegetable fat OR 180 ml (6 fl oz) oil
250 g (8 oz) Bramley apples, unpeeled, cored and grated
125 g (4 oz) mixed peel

Blackberry and Apple Jam

Stew the apples and blackberries in a pan, then mash them to a pulp. Add the sugar. Cook over a low heat, stirring constantly, until the sugar dissolves. Bring to the boil, and then boil rapidly until setting point is reached. Skim, pour into warm, dry jars and cover.

MAKES 2.5 KG (5 LB).

375 g (12 oz) cooking apples, peeled, cored and sliced
300 ml (½ pint) water
1 kg (2 lb) blackberries
1.5 kg (3 lb) preserving sugar

Raspberry and Rhubarb Jam

Wash, peel (if necessary) and cut up the rhubarb into 1 inch lengths. Wash the raspberries and add them to the rhubarb. Add the sugar. Cook over a low heat, stirring constantly, until the sugar dissolves. Bring to the boil, and then boil rapidly until setting point is reached. Skim and pour the jam into clean, warm jam jars and cover.

MAKES 2.5 KG (5 LB).

1 kg (2 lb) rhubarb
500 g (1 lb) raspberries
1.5 kg (3 lb) preserving sugar

Green Tomato and Apple Jam (Opposite)

Place all the ingredients in a large saucepan. Cook over a low heat until the sugar is dissolved, then boil rapidly until setting point is reached. Stir occasionally mashing up the bits of tomato and apple with a potato masher. Pour into hot sterilized jars and cover tightly. Keep for a few weeks before eating.

Tip: use some of the sugar to sprinkle over the cut apples whilst cutting them. To stop the apple from going brown, cover the apples with more sugar, as you put them in with the tomatoes.

Makes about 1.25 kg (2½ lb).

500 g (1 lb) green tomatoes thinly sliced
500 g (1 lb) cooking apples, peeled and chopped
625 g (1¼ lb) granulated sugar
2 tbs vinegar, cider or malt
2 tbs water

Orange Marmalade (Opposite)

Scrub and halve the oranges, squeeze the juice into a large saucepan and add the lemon juice. Slice the orange peel into long thin slices. Add the peel and the water to the saucepan. Bring to the boil, reduce heat and cook slowly for about 2 hours until the peel is soft. It should squash easily between the fingers and the liquid should be well reduced. Add sugar and stir until dissolved.

Increase the heat and bring to a full boil for about 15 minutes until setting point is reached. If the setting point has been reached then leave the marmalade to stand for 15 minutes. Stir, to distribute the peel. Leave to cool before putting into warm jars.

MAKES 3.5 KG (7 LB).

1.75 kg (3½ lb) Seville oranges
6 tsp lemon juice
3.6 l (6 pints) water
3 kg (6 lb) preserving sugar

Orange and Carrot Jam

Peel the oranges. Wash and finely shred the orange peel. Place in a preserving pan or thick-based saucepan with half of the water. Bring to the boil, strain and throw this water away. Put the oranges back into the pan with the second half of the water. Bring to the boil for 10 minutes. Add the carrots and cook for a further 10-15 minutes. If it dries, add more water. Add sugar and boil at a high temperature, stirring often with a wooden spoon, until the consistency thickens. Add lemon juice, and stir. Leave to cool and, whilst still warm, put into sterilised jars and seal them.

MAKES 2 KG (4 LB) OF JAM.

1 kg (2 lb) oranges, skinned
1 l (1¾ pints) water
500 g (1 lb) carrot, grated
500 g (1 lb) preserving sugar
juice of ½ lemon

Strawberry Jam (Opposite)

Put the strawberries into a heavy pan and cook for 5 minutes, stirring occasionally until they are soft and pulpy. Add sugar and lemon juice. Stir over a low heat until the sugar is dissolved. Increase the heat and boil rapidly until setting point is reached.

Put into sterilized jam jars and cover.

MAKES 2.5 KG (5 LB).

2.5 g (5 lb) strawberries
1 kg (2 lb) preserving sugar
juice of 1 lemon

Dried Apricot Jam

Wash the apricots under cold running water. Place them in a large mixing bowl with water. Leave to soak overnight. Next day, put the apricots and water into a large pan and add lemon juice. Cover with a lid and simmer for 30 minutes until tender stirring occasionally. Remove the lid and boil rapidly until the contents have reduced by about a third. Add in the sugar and stir until the sugar has dissolved. Cook further until setting point is reached. Pour the jam into sterilized, warm jam jars.

MAKES 2 KG (4 LB).

500 g (1 lb) dried apricots,
*   quartered*
1.8 l (3 pints) cold water
juice of 2 large lemons
1.5 kg (3 lb) granulated sugar

Paneer

Heat the milk to boiling point, then add the lemon juice or the yoghurt (add more yoghurt if necessary). As it starts to separate, lower the heat to medium for 1-2 minutes and then take the pan off the heat. Strain through a large sieve or cheesecloth. If cheesecloth is used, gather the paneer in the centre, tie a knot and put it on a flat surface. To drain off the excess water, place a heavy object, such as a large pan filled with water, on top. Cut into cubes.

The water from the paneer can be used for soups. Paneer can be frozen.

600 ml (1 pint) milk
juice of 1 lemon OR
5-6 tbs plain yoghurt

Cottage Cheese

Crumble the cold paneer and add 3-4 tablespoons of plain yoghurt.

Cottage Cheese will last for a week in the refrigerator.

Finely chop cucumber, tomato and fresh parsley. Mix with cottage cheese, salt, pepper and cumin seeds or fennel seeds. Serve on toast or in toasted sandwiches.

Paneer
3-4 tbs plain yoghurt

Yoghurt

Bring the milk to the boil in a pan. Leave to cool until just lukewarm. Mix a little of the warm milk with the yoghurt. When smooth, add to the rest of the warm milk. For the yoghurt to set, either pour it into a vacuum flask and leave to stand for 4-6 hours or into a glass or steel bowl, cover with a lid and leave to stand in a moderately warm place for 6-8 hours.

Yoghurt can be kept for up to 5 days in a refrigerator.

MAKES 600 ML (1 PINT).

600 ml (1 pint) milk
1 tbs plain yoghurt

Brahma Kumaris World Spiritual University

The Brahma Kumaris World Spiritual University is an international organisation working at all levels of society for positive change. Established in 1937, the University now has more than 8,500 centres in over 100 countries.

Acknowledging the intrinsic worth and goodness of the inner self, the University teaches a practical method of meditation that helps people to cultivate their inner strengths and values

The University also offers courses and seminars in such topics as positive thinking, overcoming anger, stress relief and self-esteem, encouraging spirituality in daily life. This spiritual approach is also brought into healthcare, social work, education, prisons and other community settings.

The University's Academy in Mount Abu, Rajasthan, India, offers individuals from all backgrounds a variety of life-long learning opportunities to help them recognise their inherent qualities and abilities in order to make the most of their lives.

The University also supports the Global Hospital and Research Centre in Mount Abu.

All courses and activities are offered free of charge.

www.bkwsu.org
www.bkpublications.com

World Headquarters

PO Box No 2, Mount Abu 307501, Rajasthan, India
Tel: (+91) 2974 - 238261 to 68, Fax: (+91) 2974 - 238883
E-mail: abu@bkivv.org

International Co-Ordinating Office and Regional Office For Europe and The Middle East

Global Co-operation House, 65-69 Pound Lane,
London, NW10 2HH, UK
Tel: (+44) 208 727 3350, Fax: (+44) 208 727 3351
E-mail: london@bkwsu.org

Africa

Global Museum for a Better World, Maua Close,
off Parklands Road, Westlands, Po Box 123, Sarit Centre,
Nairobi, Kenya
Tel: (+254) 20-374 3572, Fax: (+254) 20-374 3885
E-mail: nairobi@bkwsu.org

Australia and South East Asia

78 Alt Street, Ashfield, Sydney, NSW 2131, Australia
Tel: (+61) 2 9716 7066, Fax: (+61) 2 9716 7795
E-mail: ashfeld@au.bkwsu.org

The Americas and The Caribbean

Global Harmony House, 46 S. Middle Neck Road
Great Neck, NY 11021, USA
Tel: (+1) 516 773 0971, Fax: (+1) 516 773 0976
E-mail: newyork@bkwsu.org

Russia, CIS and The Baltic Countries

2 Gospitalnaya Ploschad, build. 1, Moscow - 111020,
Russia Tel: (+7) 495 263 02 47, Fax: (+7) 495 261 32 24
E-mail: moscow@bkwsu.org